THE CURSE OF THE INDY 500

RED ⚡ LIGHTNING BOOKS

THE CURSE OF THE
INDY
500

1958's TRAGIC LEGACY

Stan Sutton

This book is a publication of
Red Lightning Books
1320 East 10th Street
Bloomington, Indiana 47405 USA
redlightningbooks.com

The paper used in this publication meets the minimum requirements of the
American National Standard for Information Sciences—Permanence of
Paper for Printed Library Materials, ANSI Z39.48–1992.

Manufactured in the United States of America

978-1-68435-000-1 (paperback)
978-1-68435-001-8 (cloth)
978-1-68435-002-5 (ebook)

1 2 3 4 5 22 21 20 19 18 17

To Aeden and Avery

CONTENTS

ACKNOWLEDGMENTS

SINCE I FIRST HEARD A RACING ENGINE OVER THE RADIO IN 1946, THE Indianapolis 500 has continually replenished my memory bank. From my earliest days visiting the track to the last time I drove through the infield tunnel at five in the morning, the Speedway has been a home away from home.

Every new track record, every smell of methanol, even every rain delay was a trip to paradise. When I became a sportswriter, every fourteen-hour working day saw me where I wanted to be. Nothing equaled standing in Mario Andretti's pit, or asking Rick Mears a question, or listening to a race car fire up in Gasoline Alley.

I owe a lot of people for the chance to do this. Most of all my dad, who took me to the 1958 race that remains implanted in my memory. Especially to my wife, Judy, who didn't complain when I spent every Mother's Day at time trials. But also to my friends at the Speedway, who once came up with an extra parking pass when I lost mine. Also, to public relations folks such as John Love, Hank Abts, Anne Fornoro, and Tom Blattler, who got us in touch with busy drivers when we needed them.

To reporters there are two pieces of hallowed ground inside the track. One is the present media room, which has more television sets than H. H. Gregg and more room to work than the inside of Hinkle Fieldhouse. Even more precious among our memories is the cramped, smoky, and often filthy press room that preceded it. Race day it was so crowded that some reporters sat on the floor with computers on their laps.

The carpet there predated Wilbur Shaw, and late in every workday public relations rep Michael Knight would drag a large cooler of beer across the rug, striving to cool everyone's taste buds. Sooner rather than later, the Speedway staff asked him to stop because he was ruining the carpet.

Still, many Speedway employees of that day remain among my friends: Fred Nation, Bill York, Tim Sullivan, Eric Powell, Jan Shaffer, Josh Laycock, Dick Mittman, Bob Walters, Ron Green, Mai Lindstrom, and too many others to remember. Also, the press corps with writers such as Robin Miller, Curt Cavin, Dave Van Dyke, Phil Richards, Charley Hallman, Charlie Vincent, Bill Benner, Tim May, Angelique Chengelis, Mike Vega, Terry Reed, Bob Markus, Tom Reck, and Al Stilley.

Thanks to Ashley Runyon of Indiana University Press for challenging me to write this book and for her patience in overseeing it. Likewise to her colleagues: Peggy Solic, John Decker, and Rhonda Van Der Dussen. Project manager Darja Malcolm-Clarke and copyeditor John Mulvihill were true professionals.

Special thanks to Jeff O'Connor and Bryce Mayer, who welcomed me to North Vernon and made me feel at home there. And to Bill Marvel, who remembers the 1958 race and probably is the biggest racing fan I know. His help was unbelievable.

My wife, Judy, and daughter, Shari, guided me through the countless technical problems encountered by a child of the '50s.

Most of all, those of us who love racing owe an incalculable debt to those who paid the ultimate price in a race car. Godspeed to you all.

THE **CURSE** OF THE INDY 500

A Convoluted Account
of the Crash

IN THE SPRING OF 1958 THE INDIANAPOLIS 500 COULD ARGUABLY CLAIM to be one of America's top five sporting events. In the same category were the World Series, the Kentucky Derby, the next heavyweight championship fight, and probably the Rose Bowl. The Final Four basketball tournament carried less impact then, and the Super Bowl wasn't even on the horizon.

The 500, the longest and most unique race until stock cars copied the format in the '50s, prospered because of America's growing fascination with the automobile. Fans that went to races in Model T's were obsessed with speed and noise, not to mention danger. Critics of the sport, and there were many, often accused followers of attending races only to see accidents, and perhaps even fatalities. Despite 11 deaths in the first 10 years of racing at the Indianapolis Motor Speedway, crowds continued to come.

Even two world wars failed to stymie the interest, although the 500 was abandoned from 1942 to 1945, and the Speedway was overgrown with weeds. When the race resumed it was popularized by the Indianapolis Motor Speedway Radio Network. While obviously primitive, the IMS Network drew vast numbers of listeners who appeared to be mesmerized by the sound of racing engines.

There were few options available to the announcers except to occasionally give the standings, conduct a few interviews, and keep the microphones open to the sound of racing engines.

Much of the time was filled by announcers' remarks such as, "That was Ted Horn," or, "That sound was Rex Mays moving into the lead."

On May 30, 1958, thousands of cars rolled into the infield at dawn, maneuvering for a prime spot where they could see race cars go past. In those days fans were allowed to construct scaffolding alongside their cars from which to better watch the race.

As the eleven o'clock start approached, tension mounted as in no other sport. Thirty-three cars lined three abreast suddenly lurching up to speed seemed to carry the risk of military battles.

One of the first-time announcers at the 1958 race was Lou Palmer, an Indianapolis radio personality hired to announce happenings in the third corner of the 2.5-mile track. The chief announcer was the golden-voiced Sid Collins, who was supported by five subordinates around the track. When an accident occurred, it was up to this crew to describe the incident.

Being a rookie, Palmer was assigned to the third turn, where the chances of a first-lap crash were considered less likely than in the first two corners. Although drivers are warned not to try to win the race in the first turn there was more concern than usual that pole-sitter Dick Rathmann and second-fastest qualifier, Ed Elisian, might take undue chances.

Palmer, who had lived in Indiana only five years, settled into his spot outside the third-turn wall. He couldn't know how quickly bad things were to happen. Rathmann and Elisian began their duel with Rathmann jumping in front, but as the two front-runners approached the third corner Elisian pulled in front.

However, according to numerous onlookers, he failed to adequately slow for the turn and began a spin that collected Rathmann and put them both into the outside wall.

Several hundred yards into the infield a fan atop one of the scaffolds shouted to fans below, "There are cars spinning all over the third turn."

Palmer, undoubtedly overwhelmed by the scene in front of him, began a convoluted description to his radio audience:

"And we've had an accident here! Car No. 5, the Zink Special [Elisian], is the first to wreck.

"Another over the wall [Jerry Unser]! And we've got one, two, three, four, five, six cars piled up here on the northeast turn! The 54 Novi [Bill Cheesbourg] into the infield . . . Car No. 19 [Johnnie Tolen] in the infield . . . 68 [Len Sutton] now down into the infield and it's almost impossible to identify the others.

"Out of car No. 5, now, is Ed Elisian and, er, car 91 [probably 97, Rathmann] against the wall. That is all we can see at the moment.

"Further down the track there are still others. One car has left this track, Sid, and did go over the retaining wall. That's all of the information we can give you at the moment. We will check each car for you and will report on all of them as soon as we can."[1]

What Palmer didn't describe, but almost certainly saw, was the burning blue No. 4 car of popular Pat O'Connor. The crash of Elisian and Rathmann happened in front of Jimmy Reece, the third first-row starter. O'Connor, whose car started in the middle of the second row, had no place to go, and his car ran up on Reece's, rolling over in the air and landing upside down with a loud clang before stopping on its wheels. The 29-year-old O'Connor was trapped, although probably already dead, in a burning car.

Of the 15 cars involved, eight couldn't return to the race. Others continued with damaged vehicles, and only 13 completed the entire two hundred laps.

Jimmy Bryan, whose racing success peaked on dirt tracks, won his lone Indianapolis 500, but his biggest moment was spoiled by the day's tragedy.

2

A Race-Day Shootout

UNTIL 1957 THE RACE STARTED WITH CARS LINED UP ON THE MAIN straightaway in 11 rows of three abreast. But in accordance with remodeling of the Speedway this was changed in 1957 and 1958, and in each instance things did not go as intended.

The primary improvement in '57 was the construction of a new control tower at the start-finish line that replaced the outdated 30-year-old pagoda. Also, the pit lane was separated from the main straightaway by a concrete wall and grass strip that would help protect crewmen in the pits.

Race officials decided to line up the 33 cars in the pits and start them off in a single line. During the pace lap the cars would assemble in the 11-row formation. Previously, a single pace lap had preceded the flying start, but in 1957 officials added another warm-up lap, and that resulted in confusion in each of the two starts.

Elmer George, who was married to track owner Tony Hulman's daughter, Mari, ran into the back of Eddie Russo's car as the cars shuffled for a starting position, and both drivers were out of the race before it started.

George was a rookie at the Speedway in 1957 and was scheduled to start from the outside of the third row. He didn't make the race again until 1962, when he started 17th and went out after engine problems surfaced on the 146th lap. His only other 500 was in 1963, when he started in the 10th row and went out after 21 laps, finishing 30th.

George raced champ cars throughout the 1950s and won one race. In a 1962 race in Phoenix, his car broke through a chain-link fence and injured 22 spectators.[1]

Elmer and Mari had three daughters and one son, Tony George, former CEO of the Speedway and founder of the Indy Racing League.

Mari filed for divorce from Elmer on May 3, 1976, and on race day that month George went to Terre Haute, Indiana, and confronted Guy Trolinger, an alleged friend of Mari's. Early the next day George died of multiple gunshot wounds. Trolinger was cleared by a grand jury, which ruled the shooting was in self-defense.[2]

3

May Was Busting Out
All Over

IN 1958 DWIGHT D. EISENHOWER WAS PRESIDENT AND ELVIS PRESLEY was king. A postage stamp cost three cents, and schools in Little Rock, Arkansas, had been ordered to integrate. Life expectancy was a fraction short of 70 years.

The flattop haircut was still popular, and saddle oxfords were the shoe of choice for many teenagers. Kentucky had won its fifth NCAA championship, and the Yankees won the World Series in seven games. LSU, led by Billy Cannon, had been crowned as the best in college football.

A couple of hours south of Indianapolis the horse racing world was gaga over Silky Sullivan, a colt famous for coming from far behind to win races. Silky once won from 41 lengths off the pace, but in the Kentucky Derby he came in 12th out of 14 horses as Tim Tam triumphed.

In Indianapolis there were no Colts or Pacers, and only the minor league Indianapolis Indians provided professional sports. *Breakfast at Tiffany's* was a best-selling book, and *Vertigo* and *South Pacific* were popular movies. Indianapolis newspapers couldn't write enough about Connie Nicholas's shooting of her wealthy lover, Forrest Teel.

Within days of the Indianapolis 500 Charles de Gaulle was brought out of retirement to rule France, and the SS *Edmund Fitzgerald* was launched in the Great Lakes. In May large numbers of fans flocked to the track to celebrate the rite of spring and racing, a perfect marriage in Indiana.

Time trials traditionally drew the second largest crowd in sports, yielding only to race-day attendance. The Speedway never announced the size of its crowds, which probably caused the estimates to be inflated to as much as three hundred thousand on pole day.

Time trials stretched over two weekends, and in the 1950s the track's one- and four-lap qualifying records could be broken multiple times. The first-day crowd had come to see a battle for the pole that had been developing throughout the opening week of practice. It would be a duel between Ed Elisian and Dick Rathmann.

Tensions built during the week before the pole winner was determined. There was the normal speculation about what speed would be needed to win the pole and about what it would take to make the 33-car field. Each year there were fans who thought cars were going as fast as they could go at the 47-year-old Speedway.

Bill Marvel, a longtime official with the US Auto Club (USAC), vividly recalled the week before pole day.

"That thing that happened at the Speedway started that month. I remember it just as well as I can see the sun shining" Marvel recalled. "Ed Elisian and Dick Rathmann, every evening they would go out and go fast. The other guy would go out and try to go faster, it was that way all month. The two of them, every evening. And that's what led to that first lap, to that thing on the first lap of the race."

Marvel, who began part-time work at the track in 1953, said everyone could sense a potential problem.

"Of course," he said. "Jimmy Reece was caught up in front of them later that year and we lost him at Trenton. I used to run around with Jimmy, and he was like a brother whenever he'd come to the Speedway. You could see that something was going to happen. One of those guys was going to lead the first lap and that's what it amounted to. It was so obvious."[1]

Pat O'Connor made his first appearance on the third day the track was open and turned a practice lap of 143.946 mph. The four-lap track record was 145.596, set in 1956 by Pat Flaherty.

"I don't believe there's a ceiling on speed here," O'Connor said. "We should be doing 150 mph laps in a couple more years."[2]

Pat was driving for the second straight year in the Sumar Special, the same vehicle in which he won the pole in 1957. He had put the yellow Ansted-Rotary Special on the outside of the front row in 1956.

O'Connor noted that the Sumar car had received an overhaul from mechanic Ray Nichols before the race. "It's had a $5,000 tune-up and that's hardly the kind you'd get at your neighborhood gas station," O'Connor said.

The Sumar Special that O'Connor drove in 1958 was easily identified. Royal blue except for a wide white stripe down the middle, O'Connor's race car had multiple exhaust pipes extending from the engine. Chapman Root of Terre Haute was the principal owner.

Three years earlier Root had brought a car to the Speedway with a revolutionary new look. Driven by Jimmy Daywalt, the car appeared much like a sports car, with fenders front and back. However, it wouldn't get up to qualifying speed until the fenders were removed, giving the car an unfinished appearance. Nevertheless, Daywalt qualified it in the sixth row and finished ninth in the race.

Root and co-owner Don Smith used their wives' first names in labeling the car "Sumar" (Sue and Mary).

Although high winds raged the track during midweek practice sessions, a total of 31 cars were on the track one day, a high number by past standards. It was a couple of days before Jimmy Bryan brought out his car, the same one in which Sam Hanks had won in 1957. The car, designed by George Salih, had a lay-down Offenhauser engine that was a trendsetter.

Johnny Thomson, one of several contenders to win the race, was unhurt in a long slide down the straightaway during practice. Two days before pole day O'Connor had a lap at 141.6 during another busy day at the track.

Fast Friday, on the eve of pole day, saw some of the pole favorites open up. Ed Elisian appeared to have an edge after going 145.723 mph. Jimmy Reece threated to challenge him after going 144.7, and Bryan also went 144.7. No one was overlooking Dick Rathmann.

The day before pole day Rathmann turned a lap at over 147 mph, causing a near panic in Elisian's garage where Smokey Yunick officiated. Yunick vowed that Elisian would surpass Rathmann's speed, and Ed did by going 148.148 mph. But that speed wouldn't be matched when push came to shove a day later.[3]

On Saturday, May 17, Elisian wasted no time setting a new one-lap qualifying record of 146.508 mph, and he recorded a four-lap reading of 145.920. Elisian then was forced to wait to see if his tentative pole time could stand up all day. Only first-day qualifiers were eligible to sit on the pole.

Rathmann went out later and won the pole with a 10-mile speed of 145.974 mph. Rathmann's one-lap speed was slower than Elisian's. Veteran Jimmy Reece would be third quickest, followed by Bob Veith, Pat O'Connor, and Johnnie Parsons.

Once the pole was determined, it would be 13 more days before the race, enough time for Rathmann and Elisian to extract another flick of speed from their cars. Also enough time for them to concoct possible ways of beating each other around the first 2.5 miles of the race. Tension continued to build as the gates opened at 5:00 AM on race day and a crowd of some two hundred thousand entered the hallowed grounds, many of them worrying what the start of the race might bring.

The day before the 500 the 33 drivers met with the chief steward, who in 1958 was first-year official Harlan Fengler. Fengler had driven one race there, finishing 16th in 1923. Above everything else he was called on to keep the race safe.

In his meeting with the drivers Fengler pleaded with them, as had his predecessors, to not try to win the race on the first lap. He also warned drivers not to improve their positions during caution periods and not to drive consistently under the white line on the inner part of the track. Such violations, Fengler said, would result in a black flag calling the driver in for consultation. Such a penalty would result in a driver losing about two laps to the field.

O'Connor expressed optimism while being interviewed over the public address system the morning of the race. Jimmy Bryan, who would start from the inside of the third row, was favored to win, but O'Connor also received heavy support.

For the second straight year the field lined up along pit row instead of in eleven rows of three on the main straightaway. The 33 cars started rolling off pit lane onto the track itself with the intention of falling into position for the start of the race

Somehow, and with deadly consequences, the first row of Rathmann, Elisian, and Reece got ahead of the pace car. Before the race could start they had to go fast enough to circle the track, catch the other 30 cars, and squeeze past them on the narrow track before getting into the predetermined position. Confusion, and undoubtedly anxiety, reigned supreme.

Normally, drivers in the first two rows feel safer at the start than those deep in the field. There is considerably less risk in front because there are fewer cars that could lose control. Also, drivers back in the pack often have less experience and may have more trouble finding a lane in which to circumvent the first turn.

While O'Connor undoubtedly felt anxiety, he was starting in the first two rows for the third straight year. If he was worried about a Rathmann-Elisian duel, he didn't say anything publicly.

Defending champion Sam Hanks was driving the pace car, and the front row was staggered somewhat as the green flag fell. Rathmann led by about two car lengths over Elisian exiting the first turn. Elisian darted below the white line and cut into Rathmann's lead through the second turn.

Down the lengthy backstretch Elisian took the inside position and pulled even with Rathmann, moving just ahead before losing control in the third turn. The rear end of Elisian's car spun 180 degrees and slid toward the outside wall, collecting Rathmann's car. At almost the same time they hit the wall O'Connor's car began its ascent of Jimmy Reece's racer. Bob Veith, who started the race directly to the left of O'Connor, managed to get his damaged car to the pits, finishing eight positions ahead of the cars immobilized by the accident.

Rookie A. J. Foyt described the accident in his autobiography, *A. J.*:

"I saw Reece slow down, and then Bob Veith hit him, sending Reece's car directly into the path of Pat O'Connor." Foyt further wrote that O'Connor's car sailed 50 feet into the air and burst into flames when it hit the track. Doctors believe O'Connor died of a fractured skull and was dead before flames emerged.[4]

The horrifying sounds included screeching tires everywhere and the clanking of metal, including the sound of the Sumar Special hitting the track upside down. One car sent large clumps of dirt flying in all directions as it spun into the infield. Another sent a photographer scurrying for safety as it slid directly toward him.

In those days the Indianapolis Motor Speedway was unique in one regard. Because of trees and grandstands people on the front straightaway could not see what was happening on the other parts of the track. Pit crews and fans knew little about the accident other than the fact that certain cars weren't coming past them any longer.

The caution light was on almost a half hour as the debris was cleared and the race resumed. Some drivers, including Paul Russo in the popular Novi, pulled into the pits and returned to the track after lengthy repairs. He finished 18th after completing 122 laps.

After the race, chief steward Fengler admitted the start of the race was "terrible" but added his belief that the confusion on the pace lap had nothing to do with the accident.[5]

Jimmy Bryan, the dirt-track specialist, took the lead after the cars returned to high speeds and held it for 18 laps. Tony Bettenhausen, who like Bryan had started in the third row, was second and Eddie Sachs third. George Amick, a highly touted rookie, challenged and moved into third as Bettenhausen moved into the lead. Amick soon was dueling Bryant and Bettenhausen for the lead, which changed hands 14 times in the first half of the race.

Sachs contended in the opening laps but dropped out on lap 68 with transmission problems. Meanwhile, Johnny Boyd moved into position to challenge Bryan and Bettenhausen. Foyt's first 500 ended when he spun out on lap 149, and Bryant led the final 75 laps to win his only 500 in George Salih's yellow Belond AP Special.

The grimy Phoenix driver quickly lit a cigar upon driving into Victory Lane.

The rest of the top 10 had Amick, Boyd, Bettenhausen, Jim Rathmann, Jimmy Reece, Don Freeland, Jud Larson, Eddie Johnson, and Bill Cheesbourg.

There was no Yard of Bricks for the winner to kiss in 1958. The main straightaway consisted of the original brick surface, with the remainder of the 2.5-mile circuit covered with asphalt.

4

O'Connor's Eternal Home

VERNON, INDIANA, IS BY FAR THE SMALLEST COUNTY SEAT IN THE
state. Its 370 residents live surrounding a courthouse square that matches the
century-old buildings of the town. While not a city, Vernon nonetheless has
a mayor, and the town has avoided being swallowed up by North Vernon, the
city of 5,311 that almost touches Vernon's north border.

There would seem to be no reason to turn down one of Vernon's side streets
and see what's on the edge of town. But if you do, you will drive into one of the
most beautiful cemeteries in southern Indiana. It has far more souls implanted
in its green pastures than Vernon has in its population.

Narrow lanes bisect the well-kept cemetery, and if a visitor turns left at the
second lane he will spot a black headstone with a contrasting tablet centered
on the stone. It states, simply, "Pat O'Connor."

There is no middle name. No date of birth or death. No favorite scripture.
The only further identification of the occupant is a pair of thinly etched checkered flags.

Judging by his memorial Pat O'Connor was just any normal resident. There
is no information listed that says he probably was North Vernon's most popular citizen. Nothing tells you of the sorrow his friends and neighbors felt on
May 30, 1958, the day he needlessly lost his life in the Indianapolis 500.

O'Connor, who was 29, was laid to rest after a moving ceremony at the First
Baptist Church of North Vernon, which at that time was near the downtown
area and several miles from the Vernon Cemetery.

"They said when the hearse was pulling into the cemetery at Vernon the last car was leaving the church," said O'Connor's son, Jeff. "It was one of the longest processions that had ever been around here. A lot of people were lined up along State Street. In fact, I think it was even on the radio."

Only if a visitor takes the time to walk up to O'Connor's tombstone will he notice a row of weathered coins resting atop the monument. About a dozen coins, mostly quarters, lie there undisturbed.

"We don't know what's behind it, but no one takes them," Jeff O'Connor said.[1]

Pat O'Connor grew up in North Vernon, but his family moved to Indianapolis, where he graduated from high school. Shortly thereafter they moved back to North Vernon, which is located equidistant from Cincinnati, Indianapolis, and Louisville.

Pat had a thing about automobiles and racing early in his adult life, but they weren't his only fixations. According to Bryce Mayer, editor of the *North Vernon Plain Dealer & Sun,* O'Connor owned a combined hotel-restaurant in North Vernon. "The Greenleaf restaurant had a neon sign with a little racing car on it. When they tore the building down a few years ago Jeff got the sign," Mayer said.[2]

O'Connor also supplemented his income from racing by selling Chevrolets at Webster's and selling insurance.

Not far from O'Connor's grave is the final resting place of Wilbur Shaw, a native of Shelbyville, Indiana, who was a three-time winner of the Indianapolis 500 and its president prior to his death in a 1954 plane crash. Also in the area, in a triangle location with the O'Connor and Shaw graves, lies the body of Jim Hemmings, a promising sprint-car driver who was killed in 1962 at age 28. Hemmings died in a crash at Marion, Ohio, that also killed veteran Shorty Templeman.

"Jim Hemmings was a protégé of Dad, who was a protégé of Wilbur Shaw," Jeff O'Connor said. "He was a North Vernon boy. He had great potential and was just starting to get up to that level.[3]

During a memorial ceremony at a North Vernon park in 2015, Speedway historian Donald Davidson told onlookers that the Speedway had offered to make O'Connor its president at the end of the 1958 season.

"Tony [Hulman, Speedway owner] wanted Pat to replace Wilbur and take over as president of the Speedway." Davidson said. "Now wouldn't that have been something?"[4]

Pat's widow, Analice, returned to North Vernon, where she still lives with her second husband.

Interest in racing is high in North Vernon, as is typical in Indiana. Jeff O'Connor said some of his father's early races were held at "The Hole," a dirt track near Columbus, Indiana.

"Back in those days there was a lot of interest in harness racing in all the little towns, He and a buddy of his would take their jalopies and go out to this harness track and do a little racing," Mayer said.[5]

One of the few North Vernon residents still living who knew O'Connor well is Lendal Patterson. Now 94, the former auto dealer made regular trips to Indianapolis, and O'Connor would ride along and be dropped off at the Speedway. When Patterson was finished with his business, he'd pick up Pat on the way home.

"He was a guy you wanted to be with. He took that racing seriously, and he was a good family man, just an all-around good man. We lost one of the best men in town," Patterson said.[6]

Bill Marvel said O'Connor was very popular with racing fans.

"Pat was one of the better guys. He was so good with the race fans it was unbelievable," Marvel recalled. "We had the Hoosier Auto Racing fans, and he used to attend all of the meetings. We had them at the World War Memorial and he'd come up from North Vernon. When my boy was young, Pat O'Connor was his hero. Billy would call him Patto Connor. He thought his name was Patto. He was like a magnet to people because he was good looking, I think all the women liked to see him."[7]

5

The City of Railroads

IF A VISITOR DRIVES INTO NORTH VERNON AND COMES UPON A WIDE railroad crossing, he is downtown.

"City of Railroads is the nickname of this town," said Bryce Mayer, whose father was editor of the town's semi-weekly newspaper and whose shoes he now fills. In fact, the state's first railroad ran through North Vernon, linking Madison, Indiana, on the Ohio River, to Indianapolis. It still runs as the Madison Railroad.

"The main one was the B&O, now it's CSX, from Cincinnati to St. Louis. The third one was the Big Four, or New York Central, which went from north of Greensburg to New Castle and down through North Vernon to Louisville," Mayer said.[1]

In the nineteenth century as many as 90 trains passed through North Vernon daily. Legend has it that John Dillinger refused to rob a bank in the city because too many trains could prevent a quick getaway.[2]

North Vernon, which is basically attached to the smaller town of Vernon, had celebrities before Pat O'Connor became one of the nation's most famous race drivers. Author Jessamyn West was born near North Vernon. West was a cousin of Richard Nixon, who visited the city in the 1970s. West wrote *The Friendly Persuasion*, which was made into a movie, while living in a boarding house in North Vernon.[3]

North Vernon is 20 miles east of Seymour, the hometown of singer John Mellencamp and writer of the song "Small Town." Seymour is considerably larger than North Vernon.

Near the intersection of state roads 7 and 3 sits a functional one-story office building where Farm Bureau insurance agents work. In a back office sits Jeff O'Connor next to a wall filled with racing pictures of his father. His home, friends say, is a virtual museum in honor of the city's favorite son.

Jeff O'Connor was 18 months old and staying at his grandmother's house when his father was killed. His mother and aunt had gone to the race to see Pat drive the blue No. 4 Sumar Special to a possible victory. The previous year Pat had won the pole and in 1956 started from the outside of the front row.

O'Connor was driving in his fifth 500 and had finished eighth in both 1955 and 1957. O'Connor had won the Darlington 200 in 1956, the Larry Crockett Memorial at Salem Speedway in 1955, the track championship at Fort Wayne in 1954, the Illiana at Schererville in 1953, and the 1953 Sprint Car Championship.

O'Connor had said he would retire from racing and concentrate on his business interests if he won at Indianapolis.

Pat's widow, Analice, returned to North Vernon and later married Roy Stiening. "He's pretty much been my father figure since I was three or four years old," Jeff said. "They're both retired and they're enjoying life."[4]

Jeff admits he had some ambition to go into racing, but, "Pretty much out of respect for my Mom I never proceeded. She didn't want to go through what she'd already gone through. And that's understandable."

Bitterness over the accident, which was triggered by overaggressive driving by Ed Elisian, apparently is not a problem with Jeff or his mother.

"No. Obviously when you hear the stories of the Ed Elisian incident . . . things that happened . . . you just figure, yeah, it was a bad racing accident, but as they say, that's racing," Jeff said.

For the second straight year in 1958 the start was botched. The three front-row cars got behind the other 30 and had to work their way around the field before the start. Many believe the accident wouldn't have occurred with a normal start.

"If they had that messed-up a start this day and age they would have just thrown the yellow flag and gotten them all back in line," Jeff said.

Analice, whom Jeff has tried to shield from most interviews, stayed away from the Speedway for several years but now enjoys contact with a number of racing people.

"We haven't missed an Indianapolis race since 1975, which was my senior year in high school," Jeff said. "I think she figured I was too old to get into racing, but we haven't missed since. They go every year to Mari Hulman's old-timers' party. They went up for the 100th running and all the celebration. They spend a lot of time up there."

With modern technology, O'Connor's flip over Jimmy Reece's car probably wouldn't have proved fatal. The next year roll bars and flame-retardant clothing were made mandatory. Today's drivers sit much lower in the cockpit, and landing upside down probably wouldn't be fatal. Fire today can be extinguished more quickly.

While Jeff O'Connor was too young to see his father's crash, he has nonetheless been witness to some other famous fatalities, including Dale Earnhardt's at Daytona in 2001.

"It was the first and only Daytona I've ever been to," Jeff said. "It was an excellent race, but the next year the HANS device became a mandatory thing."

The HANS device fits behind the head and neck of the driver and provides protection to that area of the body.

As with many witnesses, Jeff didn't think the Earnhardt accident looked serious at first.

"It was such a slow-motion thing," he said. "We had Tony Stewart going up and down in front of cars on the backstretch prior to that and coming out unscathed. You'd have thought he would have gotten hurt. But when I saw Ken Schrader walking up to the (Earnhardt) car and turning around I thought, 'Oh, this is not good.'"

Jeff O'Connor also was a witness to perhaps the most violent one-car accident ever, when Gordon Smiley hit the third-turn wall at Indianapolis in 1982.

"I was sitting in turn 4. That was about the worst I've ever seen," he said. "I was actually in the pits prior to him going out, and they told him, 'You've got the car to get in the race,' and I could hear him chattering. He said, 'We can put this on the pole.'

"He was so in over his head. You don't drive these cars like a sprint car. I think he just tried to hammer it and he slid around, and that thing just sucked him right into the wall."

Smiley was on a warm-up lap prior to an attempted qualifying attempt. Numerous experts said Smiley overcompensated when his car's rear end began to slide outward.

Jeff also was at the Pat O'Connor Memorial race at Salem Speedway in 1990 when Rich Vogler was killed. He was mowing his yard when Dan Wheldon was injured fatally at Las Vegas in 2011. His daughter came out to inform him of the 15-car accident.

"I saw the replays and it reminded me of Dad's wreck," he said. "It has a similar launch area and the same number of cars involved. There were so many similarities it was unreal. We actually went up to the [Wheldon] memorial service."

A. J. Foyt spoke glowingly of Pat O'Connor in his autobiography, of how the veteran driver helped the rookie in 1958. Years later O'Connor's son got to meet the four-time winner on a couple of occasions.

"I met him several years ago with my wife. It was kind of funny how it happened," Jeff said.

Lori Bays O'Connor told a man outside Foyt's garage that they wanted to meet A. J., and the man replied that Foyt didn't come out to mingle with fans.

"So, she wrote on a napkin that said, 'Jeff O'Connor is out there, the son of Pat O'Connor, and he'd like to meet you.' One of the crew guys was walking through, and she said, 'Can you give this note to A. J.?'

"The guy said, 'He doesn't sign autographs very often,' and she said, 'I don't care if he signs it, I just want him to read it.'

"All these people are packed around his garage and we're standing back out of the way. He walks out and he says, 'Where's O'Connor?'"

Two years ago O'Connor and his daughter, Kristen, had a similar experience when A. J.'s son, Larry Foyt, sent word that Pat's son and granddaughter wanted to talk to him. They were invited into the garage and saw A. J. on his cell phone, whereupon Foyt said, "I'll have to call you back."

"He got to talking and he told me in that Texas voice that he almost gave up racing after Dad's accident," Jeff said. "I kind of got teary-eyed, and I said, 'A. J. I'm sure glad you didn't because you are Mr. Indianapolis.'"

6

Deadly Summer of '58

TWO OTHER DRIVERS IN THE 1958 INDIANAPOLIS 500 WOULD MEET their fate before that racing season ended. That was not an unusual number, and each May the Indianapolis 500 program would feature pictures and short tributes to those who had paid the ultimate price the prior year.

Eventually, 13 of the 33 drivers in the 1958 Indianapolis 500 would be killed in racing accidents.

Besides O'Connor, the 1958 season cost the sport Jimmy Reece and Art Bisch. Reece, a veteran of six Indy races whose race car had catapulted O'Connor to his death, died on September 28 during a 100-mile race at Trenton (NJ) Speedway. Bisch died of chest and head injuries two days after a July 4 event at Lakewood Speedway in Atlanta, Georgia.

The 1959 season would be even more deadly, resulting in the deaths of seven Indy car drivers. Three had perished in 1955, including Bill Vukovich and Jack McGrath, but the deaths of 84 in a fiery accident at Le Mans, France, was a serious blow to racing's image.

The French accident during the 24 Hours of Le Mans involved a car driven by Pierre Levegh that crashed and broke into multiple pieces close to a large bank of spectators.[1]

The death of the 31-year-old Bisch barely a month after the Indy race wiped out one of the young standouts from the racing hotbed of Phoenix, Arizona. That June 8 Bisch had enhanced his reputation by qualifying a dirt car on the pole at the Rex Mays Classic in Milwaukee, Wisconsin. Bisch dueled much of the event with veteran Tony Bettenhausen and won his only champ car race (Indy cars) under a yellow flag.[2]

Bisch had been one of the cars involved in the O'Connor crash and was officially listed in last place.

Reece, who finished sixth in the '58 Indy race, was thrown from his car when it climbed a 40-foot embankment near the concrete surface of the Trenton track. The car burst through a wooden fence, soared 100 feet through the air, and landed on a hurricane fence. Reece died en route to the hospital.[3]

Bill Marvel, a close friend of Reece, sat outside Reece's house until Jimmy's wife, Betty, came home.

"I had to tell her that he was dead. She didn't know about it," Marvel said. "She looked at me as she walked up and said, 'Well, how bad was it?' I said, 'Well, he's gone.' My wife took care of her two kids while Jack Martin, his wife, and I went with Betty—with Jimmy in the baggage compartment in a casket. We took him to Oklahoma City for the funeral."[4]

Reece had placed seventh as an Indy rookie in 1952 and started in the first two rows in 1957 and 1958. Marvel said Reece was upset at the Victory Banquet the night after the 1958 race. "He never said much to me about the accident, but I know at the Victory Banquet everyone was going on about the race. When he got up later, he said, 'We're all celebrating here but we've got to remember that we lost one of our best drivers yesterday.' He was upset with the rest of the people not wanting to address the fact that one of the best drivers got killed."

Marvel said some people actually blamed Reece because O'Connor's car went over him, but before that Reece's car was bumped into O'Connor's path by Bob Veith.

"Jimmy was a victim of circumstances. When you're going that fast with those cars all around, you're just trying to get out of the way," he continued.

7

Safety Wasn't First

AUTO RACING WAS DANGEROUS FROM ITS INCEPTION IN THE LATE nineteenth century, when the sport's hazards far outweighed its concerns for survival. In the early days, protection for the drivers, mechanics, and spectators was totally inadequate.

Participants had the mathematics to indicate the extent of the danger, but the thrills they received obviously dulled their senses. More than a century later drivers continue to believe "it will never happen to me."

When the Indianapolis Motor Speedway opened in 1909, race cars had no seat belts. Drivers, and in many cases riding mechanics, sat high in their seats, and a flipping car often proved fatal. The dirt track was full of ruts that didn't mesh with the hard rubber tires on the vehicles. Suspension on the cars was inadequate, and if the race car hit a wall there was little protection from the impact.

In addition, the drivers had virtually no experience because the sport was in its infancy. They were constantly experimenting on what part of the track was faster and safer. While Ray Harroun used a rearview mirror while winning the first 500 in 1911, most of his peers relied on "backseat drivers." Those men were mechanics who not only had to keep the oil pressure up but were required to alert the driver when cars were approaching from the rear.

In addition, crash helmets were made of leather, perhaps helpful in preventing scratches but useless when hitting another hard object at speed.

Probably because he retired after his victory, Harroun survived this tumultuous period and lived until 1968, often meeting the public with his yellow winning car and its revolutionary rearview mirror. Most race cars at that time had dual bucket seats, but Harroun sat in a single seat located in the middle of the vehicle. Harroun started the inaugural 500 in 28th place, the position determined by the order of entries. The first Indy 500 saw John Aitken beat Ralph DePalma into the first turn, and by the eighth lap Harroun's Marmon Wasp was running seventh.[1]

The 2.5-mile Speedway had been paved with bricks before the first 500, a necessity considering the hefty death toll during two years of dirt track racing. The surface remained partially brick until 1962.

Balloon racing and motorcycle racing preceded automobile racing at the Speedway, but a three-day event kicked off the latter in August of 1909. On the 50th lap of a 250-mile race, driver Wilfred Bourque's vehicle hit a rut and flipped into a ditch. Bourque and riding mechanic Harry Holcomb were trapped under the car, and both died a short time later.[2]

Two days later riding mechanic Claude Kellum died in a 300-mile race that he had begun as a riding mechanic for Johnny Aitken. Aitken's car was forced to quit because of a cracked cylinder head, and Kellum moved over to Charlie Merz's car as a mechanic. When that car flipped, Kellum died from his injuries. That same day spectators Howard Jolliff, 20, of Franklin, Indiana, and James West, 38, of Indianapolis, died when hit by a race car.[3]

Speedway officials canceled the race after 235 miles, and safety became a major concern.[4]

The next 107 years saw racing accidents at the track claim 73 lives, including 42 drivers, one motorcycle rider, 13 riding mechanics, a pit crew member, and a variety of spectators and track personnel. Victims also included at least one pilot who crashed at the Speedway during World War II when it served as a maintenance and refueling station for the 821st Aero Repair Squadron.[5]

8

Daytona Enters the Picture

IN 1953, REPORTEDLY AFTER FEELING SNUBBED DURING A VISIT TO THE
Indianapolis Motor Speedway, NASCAR czar Bill France Sr. began thinking
about building a track to showcase the stock cars that ran mostly in the southern states. Daytona International Speedway became a reality in 1959 when it
became the home of the Daytona 500, which eventually would be promoted as
the Great American Race.

Daytona International Speedway was the same length as Indianapolis, but
there were few similarities between it and the circuit built 40 years earlier in
the Midwest. First, it was a much wider track than the seemingly outdated
Indy circuit, which usually surprises first-time visitors who expect Indy to feature more racing room.

While Indianapolis is basically a rectangle, Daytona is more of a triangle
that utilizes 31-degree banking in the turns. Indianapolis has a banking of only
nine degrees in its four corners.

NASCAR's tradition is far shorter than that of the "champ cars" that ran
the races supporting the Indy 500. Stock cars first earned prominence on dirt
tracks of the South; their roots include moonshiners outrunning the law.
The first notable race was the 1950 Southern Five-Hundred, later renamed
the Southern 500, in Darlington, South Carolina. The inaugural race wasn't
sanctioned by NASCAR and was won by Johnny Mantz in a Hudson Hornet.
Mantz, from northern Indiana, had driven in two Indianapolis races.

Darlington Raceway was a 1.25-mile egg-shaped layout that later became famous as The Lady in Black and The Track Too Tough to Tame. It was the only stock car track of that length before Daytona.

One advantage for stock car racers was the availability of space for sponsor names on the cars. Years later Indy car owners often had problems obtaining sponsorships because the cars went so fast it was difficult to read the writing on them.

After Daytona was built there was a demand to host drivers who competed at Indianapolis. Although some champ car drivers were apprehensive about running such speeds on the high banks, the US Auto Club committed to a season-opening hundred-miler at Daytona on April 4, 1959.

From a racing standpoint the event was successful, as winner Jim Rathmann set a new speed record of 170.261 miles per hour, some 35 mph faster than the winning time of the prior Indianapolis 500. However, the race was marred by a spectacular crash that killed George Amick on the final lap. Amick's car hit a guard rail and catapulted end over end, killing him instantly. The front part of his car was folded like a paper wad and both front wheels came off.

Bill Cheesbourg was unhurt when he spun off the track while trying to pass Amick's car during its series of flips. Dick Rathmann also was passing when Amick hit the guard rail.

"There was so much junk in the air I could hardly see to pass," said Rathmann, who called it the worst wreck he had ever seen. To this day Indy cars haven't raced again at the track.[1]

Amick's runner-up finish in the 1958 Indianapolis race had cemented his status as a rising superstar. The 34-year old Oregon native started racing jalopies in the Northwest before moving on to midgets, where he won 16 feature events and 38 races overall. He moved up to Indy-type cars and won three races in 43 starts.[2]

Amick was named Rookie of the Year over Anthony Joseph Foyt.

The crowd for the open-wheel event was a meager 7,500, despite a field that included Foyt, Rodger Ward, Pat Flaherty, Eddie Sachs, and Tony Bettenhausen. Until Amick's accident there had been only one mishap, a spin by Dempsey Wilson. There was to have been a second hundred-mile race that day, but due to the lengthy cleanup from Amick's accident it was shortened to 50 miles.[3]

9

No Average Day at the Beach

AMERICA'S MOST UNUSUAL RACETRACK WAS LARGELY A PRODUCT OF Mother Nature herself. It was located only a few miles from the new Daytona International Speedway and was known as Daytona Beach and Road Course.

The circuit consisted of two racing surfaces, a two-mile stretch that otherwise served as state highway A1A, leading to a turn that led to another two-mile stretch along the Atlantic Ocean before turning back onto the highway. Racing on that circuit dated back to 1902 and ended in February of 1958.

Bill France Sr. operated the race surface after 1938, a year featuring two races with modest payoffs. There were three races in each of the next two years, and France was planning the 1942 event when Pearl Harbor occurred. Racing didn't resume until 1946, and NASCAR was formed in 1948. The beach track was its primary venue until the Darlington track was finished in 1950.

The first NASCAR-sponsored race was in 1949 at Charlotte Motor Speedway in North Carolina, and the second event was at the beach circuit. The July event featured 28 cars and a multitude of stock car veterans such as Curtis Turner, Buck Baker, Marshall Teague, and Tim Flock.[1] The annual races continued there until 1958, when pole-sitter Paul Goldsmith won. Cars continued to race on the sand part of the track until 1961.

Goldsmith and Teague were versatile drivers who had success both in champ cars and stock cars. Both were at Indianapolis in 1958, and Goldsmith qualified 16th in the 500 while Teague failed to make the field. Goldsmith was involved in the first-lap crash in which Jerry Unser sailed over his car and landed on the far side of the track's outside wall. A smear of rubber from Unser's tire was left on Goldsmith's helmet.

Teague was a native of Daytona Beach and was nicknamed King of the Beach for his performance there. He raced in the Indianapolis 500 three times, with a top finish of seventh in 1957. He was more competitive in NASCAR, winning seven races of the 23 in which he competed from 1949 to 1952.[2]

Teague helped fellow Daytona Beach resident Smokey Yunick become a legend as a racing mechanic. Teague drove a Hudson Hornet, the most famous stock car of its day, after walking unannounced into Hudson's Michigan office and selling the company on corporate sponsorship.[3]

On February 11, 1959, Teague was testing his reconfigured champ car at Daytona International Speedway, vying for a closed-circuit speed record, when his Sumar Special spun out of control and Teague was thrown onto the track. The 37-year-old Daytona legend was killed instantly.[4]

The first Daytona 500 was run 11 days later.

10

Champion of the Dirt

AFTER HIS STAR PEAKED AT INDIANAPOLIS, TWO-TIME WINNER BILL Vukovich confined his racing to paved tracks and bypassed events on the various dirt tracks of the champ car circuit. Vuky had the reputation of a hard-charger, which helped him win the 500 in 1953 and 1954 and come within eight laps of winning in 1952.

Vukovich thought the dirt tracks were too dangerous, and the statistics would seem to prove him right. However, paved tracks were not without danger. Vuky was killed in the 1955 Indy 500 in a multiple-car accident on the backstretch.

In the 10-year period between the resumption of champ car racing and Vuky's death, dirt track accidents were fatal to such IndyCar legends as Ted Horn and Rex Mays. Neither of those two popular drivers ever won at Indy, but Horn didn't finish worse than fourth in his last nine races there. Mays's highest finish was second, but he sat on the pole four times.

Horn and Mays died in races on tracks usually used for horse racing. Horn was killed in 1948 at the DuQuoin State Fairgrounds in Illinois on the track that once hosted the Hambletonian Stakes horse race. Mays died a year later on the Del Mar Fairgrounds track in Southern California, where the ponies often attracted celebrities from Hollywood.

Even in 1949, there were conflicts about safety in racing. Mays didn't wear a seat belt, believing a driver was safer being thrown from a car than being constricted inside it. When his car flipped, he was thrown onto the dirt and hit by several trailing cars.

Safety barriers on the horse racing tracks left something to be desired, as they did at most tracks of that day. A primary danger of the dirt tracks, most of which were a mile in length, were the ruts that developed in the surface during the racing. If a front tire hooked onto one of the ruts, the car would lurch in a different direction and occasionally begin flipping.

In the 1950s nobody could drive a car on a dirt track better than Jimmy Bryan.

A song was even written about the skills of the Phoenix racer, who was beginning to get a reputation as a specialist who couldn't win on asphalt. His 1958 victory in the 500 changed that.

Bryan had a muscular body with movie star looks that personified his western roots. He kept his hair short and seldom was seen without a cigar. He drove champ cars, stock cars, and sports car with similar success. The champ car races were largely staged on dirt, and Bryan won three national championships in the mid-1950s under the auspices of, first, the AAA and then the US Auto Club. He made 72 starts in the Indy cars, winning 23 and posting 54 top-10 finishes.[1]

Bryan raced eight times at Indianapolis and was runner-up to Vukovich in 1954, after which Jimmy's toughness was never questioned. He finished second driving a dirt track car with broken suspension. At that time the Speedway's main straightaway was paved with 40-year-old bricks that rocked Bryan's body the entire race.

Bryan was sixth at Indy as a rookie in 1952 and finished third in 1957. He led a total of 216 laps among the 1,411 he ran at the Speedway.

Another hazard awaited Indy drivers in those days. In 1953 track temperatures reached 130 degrees and several starters required relief drivers. Tragically, driver Carl Scarborough died of heat exhaustion. The Speedway's attempt to avoid such occurrences included seeking better ventilation on the race cars.

11

How Fast Is Too Fast?

ONE PHRASE GOES BACK ALMOST TO THE FIRST AMERICAN AUTOMOBILE race. People said it when cars were going 70 miles an hour, continued to say it when speeds reached 100, and sang the same song when speeds hit 230 at Indianapolis.

It goes something like this: Cars are going as fast now as they possibly can go.

The late Bill Cheesbourg, who drove in the 1958 race, once said, "Old-timers told me they paid $6 to see Barney Oldfield zoom down the Speedway stretch at 60 miles an hour. People flocked to see that because it was generally believed that man could not breathe at 60 miles an hour."[1]

No matter how racing promotors try to slow down the cars, the engineers who build them find ways for them to go faster. Tire manufacturers have advanced the rubber so much that cars seem to be riding on rails. Aerodynamics are so advanced that through "ground effects" wind pushes the car down like an upside-down airplane. The athleticism of the drivers has advanced so that they feel confident going into 90-degree turns while not letting up on the accelerator.

Still, there are times when even the drivers believe speeds have gotten too fast. Never was this belief as prevalent as in 1957 when the Race of Two Worlds was staged on the high banks of a 2.5-mile circuit in Monza, Italy. It was supposed to be an exhibition featuring drivers and cars from the United States against those from Europe. More accurately, it was a "pedal to the metal" test of courage over a track that had more bumps than a Minnesota highway after a hard winter.

The fastest qualifier at Indianapolis in 1957 was Paul Russo at 144.817 mph. On the first day of qualifying at Monza, Tony Bettenhausen toured the high banks at 177.045. There was a legitimate concern about the high speeds.

The inaugural Race of Two Worlds featured ten American drivers against three Jaguars from Great Britain and a Ferrari and Maserati from Italy. The Europeans represented Formula One, but the remainder of their peers boycotted the race.[2]

Rules were established calling for a flying start rather than a standing start favored by the European drivers. Instead of the continuous five hundred miles of Indy, Monza was to be run in three 63-lap segments, with intermissions of one hour to allow repairs to be made. The winner would be the driver who finished all three heats with the highest average speeds.

Jimmy Bryan won the first heat, followed by Pat O'Connor and five Americans: Andy Linden, Eddie Sachs, Troy Ruttman, Johnnie Parsons, and Ray Crawford. Bryan also won the second heat, which helped him become the overall winner. He was followed by Ruttman, Parsons, and Crawford. However, the bumpy track had begun to leave its mark. Sachs's car was stopped by broken cam housing bolts, Linden's car was sidelined by a cracked frame, O'Connor's had a split fuel tank, and Bob Veith was ousted by a steering problem on the first lap.

After the hour of repairs Ruttman edged Bryan to win the third heat, with Parsons third. Bryan was declared the overall winner, good for a $30,000 check.[3]

With no serious injuries occurring, the Race of Two Worlds was run again in 1958. Jim Rathmann won all three heats, while Bryan was a close second based on total points. Again, Monza was tough on machinery; the 1958 race saw the following breakdowns: Sachs, broken connecting rod; Don Freeland, broken cam gear; Rodger Ward, broken torsion bar; Phil Hill, broken magneto; Johnny Thomson, broken crankshaft; A. J. Foyt, broken crankshaft; Ruttman, broken fuel line; and Juan Manuel Fangio, broken pump.[4]

Veith probably had the scariest moment when he lost a wheel.

The Monza track remained a part of the Formula One road course until 1961 and ceased to be used for racing in 1969. Portions of it can be seen in the movie *Grand Prix*. It currently sits in a decaying state.[5]

12

O'Connor Victim of Jinx?

WHO KNOWS WHERE CURSES GAINED ACCEPTANCE AS WORTHY OF OUR recognition. Did they start with chain letters or simple superstitions such as, Don't step on the foul line, or Don't wear number 13? Can the Chicago Cubs really blame more than a century of frustration on a billy goat?

Whatever, a good curse always is good for conversation, and Pat O'Connor's death became somewhat of a national "curse." It is called the *Sports Illustrated* cover jinx, and the magazine has done all it can to perpetuate its reputation.

Over the more than six decades *Sports Illustrated* has been published, dozens of athletes shown on its cover have encountered trouble within a short time. Some cases simply involve slumps, injuries, or upset losses, but there is nothing frivolous about the O'Connor curse.

O'Connor, who was one of the favorites in the 1958 Indy 500, was the cover boy for *Sports Illustrated* the week before the race. Four days later he was gone. In a similar mode, 1955 Indy winner Bob Sweikert was killed three weeks after he made the magazine's cover.

Among the magazine's jinx listings are skier Jill Kilmont, who was paralyzed from the neck down a week after she was on the cover. Figure skater Laurence Owen was featured on the cover as "America's most exciting girl skater." Two days later she was among US skaters who perished in a plane crash.

Not all of the alleged curses are as serious. Oklahoma's football team lost to Notre Dame the week after the magazine promoted the Sooners' 47-game winning streak on its cover.[1]

13

Jerry Unser,
Unlucky Trendsetter

THE INDIANAPOLIS 500 CLAIMS A LONG LIST OF FAMILIES WHO HAVE sent multiple sons, brothers, and other kinfolk into the dangers of racing. The names include Foyt, Andretti, Vukovich, Bettenhausen, Russo, Mears, Whittington, Rathmann, Ruttman, Parsons, Carter, Rahal, and Sneva,

But none has produced as many winning drivers as have the descendants of Jerry Sr. and Mary Unser of Albuquerque, New Mexico. Their son Al is among three men who have won four Indy 500s. His brother, Bobby, has three victories in the 500. Al's son, Al Jr., captured two of the races.

One wonders how many their older brother, Jerry Jr., might have added had he not been killed in 1959.

The Unser family migrated from Switzerland and settled first in Colorado Springs, Colorado, at the foot of Pikes Peak. It was there they developed an interest in automobiles and motorcycles and were pacesetters in driving them to the peak of the famed mountain.

Jerry Unser Jr. was the fifth member of the 1958 Indy field to lose his life in a race car. Pat O'Connor had died at the Speedway, Art Bisch barely a month later at Lakewood Speedway in Georgia. Jimmy Reece perished in September at Trenton Speedway, and George Amick was killed at Daytona in April of 1959. Marshall Teague, who had been entered at Indianapolis but failed to qualify, also died in a crash the following February.

Jerry Unser's only Indianapolis race saw his car flip over the outer wall on the first lap. Most spectators probably felt his chances of survival were slim, but he had no life-threatening injuries and was awarded 31st place among the 33 drivers. Unser wasn't as fortunate the following May when he died of injuries in a crash during a practice session.[1] The 26-year-old left a wife and two sons, one of whom, Johnny, raced in five Indy events.

Known as an aggressive child and a star wrestler in high school, Jerry learned to drive in a Model A Ford and showed an aptitude toward going fast. He, Bobby, and Al became known across the Southwest for their skill on short tracks. Jerry was stationed in the Navy in Hawaii in 1952 and became a fan favorite in the islands. In 1955 he finished fourth in a race up Pikes Peak. Jerry also won the 1957 US Auto Club's stock car championship.

Shortly after his only Indy event in which he suffered a dislocated shoulder, he returned to Pikes Peak and suffered a broken nose when he rolled his car. Back in Indianapolis for the 1959 race, he hit the wall and was badly burned. He held on for 17 days before his injuries and pneumonia claimed his life.[2]

Jerry Jr., who was a twin, was born in 1932, two years before Bobby. Al came along in 1939. As good as Jerry was at Pikes Peak, Bobby was even more successful, winning six straight among his 13 championships at the hill climb.

When Jerry Unser arrived in Indianapolis for the 1959 race, he was met at the airport by Bill Marvel, then spent the night in the Marvel home. "He was living with me the night before he got killed. He slept in one of my boy's beds," Marvel said.

After the fire in O'Connor's car in 1958, the USAC ordained fire-retardant clothing for the 1959 race, but as Marvel said, "It was good for about thirty seconds in a fire."

"My wife washed his uniform in the washer and dried it. We had a fifty-five-gallon drum of chemical and dipped the uniform in it."

Marvel said he and Unser went to the track and, on arriving, he asked Jerry if he had gotten his uniform. Jerry replied, "No, we're not going to run fast today."

However, Unser was wearing the uniform when he hit the wall coming out of the fourth turn.

"What killed him were little flesh burns over his uniform where it burned through, those little burns, plus the bruises he got from hitting the wall," Marvel said.[3]

Bobby Unser's first Indianapolis race was in 1963, when he crashed and finished last in the popular Novi. His second Indy was more eventful, although in a horrible way, when he was involved in the fiery accident that killed Eddie Sachs and Dave MacDonald. That 32nd-place finish was followed by four top-10 finishes in the next five years, including his first Indy victory in 1968 when he outlasted the turbine-powered cars driven by Joe Leonard and Graham Hill.

Bobby Unser raced in 19 Indianapolis 500s, also winning in 1975 and in 1981, which provided the biggest controversy in Speedway history. On the 149th of 200 laps Unser left his pit during a caution period and passed eight cars during the caution, while Mario Andretti passed two cars. Unser and Andretti were running one-two at the time of the caution.

Unser was declared the winner but the following day was stripped of the victory and Andretti was upgraded to first place. Five months later following a lawsuit, Unser was reinstated as the winner.[4]

Two years after his brother won the 500, Al Unser led 190 of the 200 laps for his first Indy victory. During 1970 he won 10 times on oval, road, and dirt tracks to capture USAC's national championship. He repeated his Indy victory in 1971 and finished second to Mark Donohue in 1972. Between 1967 and 1988 Al Unser finished in the top seven 13 times at Indianapolis. He dominated the 1978 field for his third victory.

Unser had the reputation of being a driver who could take care of his car, rather than a hard-charger whose machinery failed during the race. In 1987 he wasn't even expected to be in the field but wound up winning in a Roger Penske car. Penske had Rick Mears, Danny Sullivan, and Danny Ongais in his stable, but Ongais suffered a serious concussion in a crash during a practice session and was ruled out of the competition. Unser drove a car that had been on display at a hotel and won after Andretti's car dropped out late in the race and Roberto Guerrero's stalled leaving his pit.

Al Unser Jr. made his Speedway debut in 1983, when he was suspected of blocking eventual winner Tom Sneva to prevent him from catching his father, who was leading the race. Junior—or as he often was called, Little Al—soon contended for higher honors and captured two International Race of Champions titles and was on a team that won two 24 Hours of Daytona titles.[5]

Al Jr. finished fourth, third, and second before capturing his first Championship Auto Racing Team title in 1990. In 1989 Al Jr. and Emerson Fittipaldi were dueling for the Indy 500 win when they touched wheels on the next to last lap and Unser struck the wall hard. He climbed out of his car and gave Fittipaldi the thumbs-up sign on the next lap.

Three years later Al Jr. beat Scott Goodyear to the checkered flag by 0.043 of a second to win his first 500. He added a second victory in 1994.

14

The Good and Bad
of Ed Elisian

ED ELISIAN IS REMEMBERED MOSTLY FOR TWO THINGS. ONE SHOWS HIM as a courageous man who risked his life while trying to save a friend. The other shows him as a foolhardy race driver whose selfishness cost the life of an innocent man.

Both are accurate assessments, but the stronger memory of this controversial Californian is the negative one. Almost universally Elisian is blamed for starting the first-lap accident that killed Pat O'Connor.

In his five races at the Speedway Elisian never led a lap, which was his immediate goal in 1958 when he started in the middle of the first row, inside pole-sitter Dick Rathmann and Jimmy Reece. Indy drivers always are cautioned about trying too hard to lead at the start, but these words fell on deaf ears in Elisian's case.

Rathmann led the 33-car assault on the first corner, but Elisian remained determined to be first after one lap. On the backstretch he pulled even with Rathmann, who was on the outside. Elisian moved ahead of Rathmann but failed to lift the accelerator soon enough to negotiate the third turn. His car started to slide, collecting Rathmann and sending both into the third-turn wall.

The 31 cars in their wake had nowhere to go, some of them sliding into the infield, some hitting other cars, one climbing over the outside wall. O'Connor, who started directly behind Elisian, ran up over Reece's car and flipped. O'Connor's Sumar Special hit the track upside down, then stopped on its wheels and caught fire, killing the popular Hoosier native.

Three years earlier another horrible crash occurred at Indianapolis. Two-time defending champion Bill Vukovich also had come up on an accident with nowhere to go. Much like O'Connor, Vukovich flipped over another car and caught fire. Elisian, a close friend of Vukovich, stopped his car on the track and ran across the racing surface in an attempt to rescue the still-trapped Vuky.

Elisian also was criticized by fellow drivers after he dueled with Jim Davis in a sprint car race at New Bremen, Ohio, in June of 1958 in which Davis sustained fatal injuries.[1]

Elisian was indirectly involved in the fatal crash of 1955 Indianapolis winner Bob Sweikert. At Salem (Indiana) Speedway in June of 1956, Sweikert's sprint car was dueling with Elisian's when it crashed over a guard rail.[2] Sweikert suffered a fatal skull fracture. Elisian was exonerated because their cars had not touched.[3]

Elisian and Rathmann shied away from reporters as the 1958 Indy race continued. Rick Johnson of the *Indianapolis Times* was among writers who approached the pair in the pits.

"Get out and leave me alone," Elisian snapped, according to Johnson's article.

Hours later, with the race over, Elisian sat in a garage and struggled to get out words.

"I saw Rathmann shoot across at the crossover," he said, "and I knew if he got in front there he'd be the devil to catch. So I stayed right on it, thinking there was enough room to make it . . . then the car started going every which way and I knew I'd lost it."

At that point one of his crew members approached, saying, "Cheer up, Eddie. They can't hang you."[4]

A day later as Rathmann recovered from a dislocated shoulder in Methodist Hospital, Johnson recalled Rathmann softening his stance against Elisian, whom he had earlier blamed for the accident.

"He just didn't use his head and got carried away," the pole-sitter said. "I don't have any hard feelings toward him today. I told Ed a day or two before the race that we had the best cars and chances we'd ever had and we could both make a lot of money if he'd use his head."[5]

Elisian's John Zink Special received superficial damage in the O'Connor wreck but didn't return to action. The car had a lost grill, a bent tailpipe, and a small kink in the frame.[6]

Two weeks before the race Elisian was arrested for speeding on West Sixteenth Street in the town of Speedway, Indiana.

Exactly 15 months after O'Connor was killed, Elisian died in a race at the Milwaukee Mile in Wisconsin. He was the sixth driver from the 1958 Indianapolis 500 to die in a racing accident.

Bill Marvel was at the Milwaukee Mile when the accident occurred.

"Elisian ended up getting killed like Vukovich in Milwaukee. He ended up upside down and was trapped under there and they couldn't put the fire out," Marvel said. "I watched and you could see his hand still trying to push the car up. Jimmy Bryan was trying to run across the track and, for some reason, they didn't stop the damn race. The people up at Milwaukee didn't have any fire equipment or anything."[7]

15

Journeymen Drivers
Also Victimized

DEATH ON THE RACING TRACK WASN'T ALWAYS PRECEDED BY SUCCESS. For years many believed that fatalities most frequently claimed the successful drivers. True, former Indy 500 winners Floyd Roberts, George Robson, Bill Vukovich, Jim Clark, Bob Sweikert, and Dan Wheldon were killed racing. Then too, some who were in the early stages of their careers, including O'Connor, Amick, and Greg Moore, also were killed.

But in far too many cases, with far too little fanfare, journeymen or aspiring champions had their ticket punched by the Grim Reaper. Dick Linder, Bob Cortner, and Van Johnson were such victims in 1959. That season would also claim Marshall Teague, Jerry Unser, Ed Elisian, and George Amick.

Linder died April 19 at Trenton, New Jersey, when he tried to avoid the spinning car of Indy veteran Don Branson. His car penetrated a guard rail, rolled over, and the 36-year-old Linder died of a broken neck.

A native of Pittsburgh, Linder had recorded more than 110 victories at various tracks in Pennsylvania. Besides racing in US Auto Club events, Linder drove in 28 NASCAR events over a seven-year period, with three wins and eight additional top-10 finishes. His last NASCAR race was in 1956 on the beach course at Daytona.[1]

Linder was killed in the same race car in which Johnson would be killed exactly three months later. The same car carried Hugh Randall to his death three years after that.[2]

Johnson and Cortner both were rookies at Indianapolis but would fail to make the field. Johnson died in a third-lap accident at Williams Grove Speedway. It came one month after his only win at the famed Langhorne Speedway.[3]

Cortner's death occurred May 19, 1959, on the Indianapolis track, where on the previous day he had passed his rookie test. Onlookers said Cortner was driving in a heavy crosswind and said that condition contributed to his car hitting the wall. Cortner's face struck the steering wheel and apparently led to internal bleeding. He died that evening of "massive head injuries."[4]

16

Death Common at Langhorne

LANGHORNE!

The mere name suggests an Old West location, perhaps the name of a saloon in Dodge City. Instead, she lay in eastern Pennsylvania, a circle of devastation where racing drivers would cast their fate and sometimes meet it head-on.

Langhorne. Where the most caustic nickname in sports, Puke Hollow, was an apt description.

Macho men challenged her with an unmatched, and often unwarranted, bravery. Equally viral studs showed their real strength by backing off when she beckoned.

From the sky she resembled a large crop circle. At ground level she was an unpaved road that tore up race car suspensions and shattered men's nerves. She had more ruts than the Chisholm Trail, and drivers never knew which one had their name on it.

Langhorne? She was no lady.

Fortunately, she is gone now, no longer there to try men's souls and sometimes claim them. One of the greatest safety measures taken by the sport was to plow away Puke Hollow and all her subsidiaries.

The one-mile dirt track was built in 1926, just in time for the Great Depression. It closed in 1971 after becoming part of the dateline on numerous newspaper obituaries. Great ones died there, and other great ones were just lucky.

Langhorne played no favorites. She was challenged by champ cars, stock cars, and even motorcycles. She was almost a perfect circle, and for race drivers it was one long power slide in which the back of the car slid outward and almost never did the vehicle point directly forward. Vision was poor, and the ride through Puke Hollow, which was the drivers' name for a rut-filled section of the track, was a thrill ride without rails.

Actually, more drivers died at the Indianapolis Motor Speedway than at Langhorne, but Indy had no ruts and far more miles were run there. In the days before *SportsCenter*, fans waited for the Monday morning newspaper to see if Langhorne, or one of her dirt track sisters, had claimed another victim.

Langhorne received a face-lift in 1965, when the circle was reconfigured to one with a "D" shape that included a straightaway. The dirt was paved with asphalt, but as urban sprawl closed in on the track it was sold.[1]

A historical marker on the old racing site reads, "Opened in 1926, this circular one-mile dirt track was known as the 'Big Left Turn.' It hosted a NASCAR inaugural race in 1949. Notable drivers Doc Mackenzie, Joie Chitwood, Rex Mays, Lee Petty, Dutch Hoag, A. J. Foyt, and Mario Andretti raced here in stock, midget, sprint, and Indy cars. Langhorne was reshaped as a 'D' and paved in 1965, The National Open Championship run here was regarded as the 'Indy of the East.' Final race was held in 1971."[2]

Champ cars ran under the auspices of the American Automobile Association (AAA) until 1956, when that sanctioning body pulled out and the US Auto Club began supervising events. Former Indianapolis winners who also won races at Langhorne included Wild Bill Cummings, Kelly Petillo, Bill Holland, Johnnie Parsons, Jimmy Bryan, A. J. Foyt, Mario Andretti, Gordon Johncock, and Al and Bobby Unser.

"That was the most dangerous, most treacherous, most murderous track there ever was. Nobody liked it and the ones who said they did were lying," said Bobby Unser.[3]

L. Spencer Riggs, author of *Langhorne! No Man's Land*, called the track a man-maker and man-breaker. Driver Paul Russo told Riggs that Langhorne "gave me butterflies the size of B-29s." Jimmy Daywalt told Riggs, "I never saw so many guys go on their head so hard and so quick. I didn't want any part of that joint."

According to Riggs, Langhorne's victims included nearly two dozen drivers and perhaps another dozen motorcyclists, flaggers, and spectators.[4]

When racing fans went about picking the toughest drivers, they started with Jimmy Bryan and listed Mike Nazaruk as No. 1-A. Nazaruk had proved his toughness before he climbed into a race car, having served in the Marine Corps in the battles of Guadalcanal and Guam. He was nicknamed Iron Mike, and he was a star at anything from midget race cars to champ cars. While on the battlefield he had vowed to become a race driver if he survived World War II.

He won more than 20 featured events in midgets and as an AAA driver in 1959 captured 14 features, including the popular Night Before the 500 in Indianapolis. Mike finished second to Lee Wallard in the 1951 Indy 500, then was fifth in 1954.

Nazaruk went to Langhorne for a sprint car race on May 1, 1955. On the 17th lap, possibly while he was adjusting his goggles, his car leaped over a fence and hit a tree, killing him instantly. He was 34.[5]

Racing people approached the 1955 Indianapolis 500 with trepidation, having already lost two popular drivers before the Speedway opened for practice. A few weeks before Nazaruk's crash, Langhorne had also claimed the life of Larry "Crash" Crockett. Crockett had been co-Rookie of the Year after coming in ninth in the 1954 Indy.

The 1955 racing season continued with tragedy. On May 16 Manny Ayulo crashed head-on into the southwest turn wall at Indianapolis and died later of his injuries. Then two-time winner Bill Vukovich was killed in the 1955 race.[6]

Jimmy Bryan went into semi-retirement following his victory at Indianapolis, but racing was his life and he still had the urge to go fast. So, when Rodger Ward decided against racing at Langhorne June 19, 1960, Bryan agreed to take over his ride. It was to be a one-race deal in the Leader Card Special, expertly prepared by ace mechanic A. J. Watson.

Bryan qualified second fastest and started the race on the outside of the front row. But on its first lap Bryan's car hooked onto a rut in Puke Hollow and flew an estimated 55 feet into the air.[7]

Bobby Grim told L. Spencer Riggs that he drove under the flipping car. "It kept getting bigger and bigger, like an airplane coming down for a landing," Grim said.[8]

Bryan's flipping car landed on him several times before stopping on its right side. Bryan was dead at age 34.

17

The Short Career
of Bobby Ball

IN THE MAJORITY OF RACING FATALITIES THE DRIVER IS KILLED
instantly. In the case of Bobby Ball, fate was not so kind.

Ball was a product of the racetracks around Phoenix, Arizona, a hotbed of
racing in the Southwest. He was born five months before Jimmy Bryan and was
raised by his grandmother after his parents died when he was one. Bothered
by his love of cars and motorcycles, she enrolled him in a military school as a
teenager in an attempt to get him focused on something else.

Nonetheless, Ball began racing roadsters and midgets and won the Arizona
State Midget Association title in 1949 and 1950. He progressed so quickly that
he earned a ride in the 1951 Indianapolis 500, qualifying ninth fastest and finishing fifth. The following year he went out with gear problems after thirty-
four laps.

Ball won the American Automobile Association race in San Jose, California, in November of 1952 and the following January was involved in a crash
at Carrell Speedway in Los Angeles. The accident left him with serious head
injuries, and he was in a coma for 14 months before dying.[1] For many years
a championship race at Phoenix International Raceway was named in his
honor.

18

Speedway Claims Bettenhausen

THE INDIANAPOLIS MOTOR SPEEDWAY STOOD INACTIVE DURING World War II because the nation could ill afford providing gasoline for entertainment when it was being rationed to the public. Whether the weed-infested track would even open again was in question, and it might not have without being sold to Anton Hulman Jr., a Terre Haute, Indiana, businessman.

Three-time winner Wilbur Shaw was instrumental in the sale and became the post-war president of the Speedway. There was major work to be done before the next 500 in 1946. In those days the grandstands were mostly wooden, and many board seats had to be replaced and painted. Automobile parts were scarce, and old racing equipment hadn't been used in five years.

It took time to get fuel to the Speedway, which meant drivers had to bring their own. Basic 91 octane sold for 21.2 cents a gallon.

Weather interrupted time trials. Rookie Tony Bettenhausen was the slowest of three qualifiers during a makeup session on Monday, May 20. However, Bettenhausen got another chance on Tuesday after his qualified car broke a camshaft. Tony went out in a backup car and qualified at 123.094 mph, to start in the middle of the ninth row. In the race Bettenhausen finished 20th when a rod broke after 47 laps.[1]

A number of drivers who had raced before the war didn't return when the track reopened. Eight rookies were in the 1946 field, but only Bettenhausen and Jimmy Jackson (six Indy appearances) became 500 regulars.

Tony became a huge crowd favorite while competing in 14 Indianapolis races and winning the national championship in 1951 and 1958. His career saw him win 21 times in champ cars while finishing in the top 10 on 74 occasions.

Bettenhausen suffered severe head injuries in October of 1950 after locking wheels with another car in a race in Sacramento, California. A spectator was killed and two others injured. After the '51 season he announced his retirement from all racing except Indy. However, before the '54 season he opted to return to a full schedule but was critically injured in a midget car race in Chicago.[2]

Bettenhausen recovered sufficiently to race at Indianapolis in 1955, although using Paul Russo as a co-driver. They finished second to Bob Sweikert, making this one of Tony's five top-10 finishes at Indy.[3]

In May 1961, by all appearances Bettenhausen had his best chance of achieving every driver's biggest dream. Tony's car was turning in the fastest laps of the month, and he looked like the favorite to capture the pole position.

On Friday, May 12, one day before competition for the pole, Bettenhausen offered to take Paul Russo's car on a test run because Russo had been struggling with the handling. During the run the Stearly Motor Freight Special smashed into the outside wall in the main straightaway and rolled 325 feet atop the concrete barrier while tearing out catch fencing above the wall. The car came to rest on a grassy area near Grandstand A, with Bettenhausen trapped inside.

Investigators determined that an anchor bolt had fallen off the front radius rod support, which allowed the front axle to twist and misalign the front wheels. When the brakes were applied, the car turned right.

Fellow driver Eddie Sachs was watching. "I saw Tony heading for the wall. I watched until it was over. Then I sat down and cried like a baby."[4]

19

Tony's Legacy Continues

THE BETTENHAUSEN FAMILY WOULD CONTINUE TONY'S PURSUIT OF a victory at the Speedway, yet there would be further tragedies and disappointments. Tony and Valerie Bettenhausen had three sons, Gary, Merle, and Tony Jr., and all followed in their father's footsteps.

"I remember the day he died, May 12, 1961. I was 17 years old," Merle said. "When they told me what happened I was very upset, but I remember listening to the race that year and saying to myself that I still want to drive in the Indy 500 someday."

Merle became a race driver, but his career was curtailed after he lost his right arm in a crash in Michigan in July of 1972. Exactly 11 months later he was racing again.

"I really didn't know what it would be like driving one-handed. It turned out much more comfortable than I anticipated. I found out I was doing 90 percent of my driving left-handed," he said.

Describing the accident, Merle said, "I apparently lost control and hit the guard rail. My car caught fire and hit the wall. I was in the car one minute and 15 seconds and tried getting out while it was still in motion, but it hit the wall again. That's when my arm was severed."[1]

Merle's older brother, Gary, would make his Indy debut in the 1968 race, joining Billy Vukovich as a second-generation driver in the race. Gary went on to win 37 midget races, which led to Roger Penske putting Gary in a car for the 1972 Indianapolis race.

Gary took the lead on the 30th lap and was dominant for most of the race. Suddenly his car slowed and he finished 14th.

Two years later Gary crashed in a dirt car at Syracuse, New York, seriously damaging his right arm. Penske had not wanted him in that kind of race and fired him from his Indy ride.[2] Gary raced in 16 more 500s, with only modest success, and died in 2014 at age 72.

"It was so natural to become friends with him," said Mario Andretti. "He was a great ambassador of the sport. He was told to leave the sprint cars and dirt cars alone, but he said, 'I'm a racer. I'm gonna race.'"[3]

Tony Bettenhausen Jr. was 10 years old when Tony Sr. died, so he received less direct influence from his father than did his brothers. Still, Tony rose to prominence as a champ car driver and owner.

Tony made 11 starts in the 500, with a best finish of seventh in his rookie year. Tony Jr. also competed in 33 NASCAR events, mostly in the 1970s, and as a car owner he helped launch the Indy car career of three-time 500 winner Helio Castroneves.

Tony was married to Shirley McElreath, the daughter of former driver Jim McElreath. Both Tony and Shirley died in a small plane crash over Harrison County, Kentucky, on Valentine's Day 2000. Also killed were business associates Russ Roberts and Larry Rangle. They were returning from Homestead, Florida, where a car-testing session had been held, and were en route to Indianapolis. The plane landed at Tri-City Airport in Blountville, Tennessee, and after leaving there went down about 30 miles north of Lexington, Kentucky.[4]

20

Check Out Those Helmets

WHEN PAT O'CONNOR BEGAN RACING, HIS PROTECTION PACKAGE WAS sadly inadequate. From the first days of the sport, drivers were almost as exposed as motorcycle riders. Even in the 1950s their helmets resembled a cereal bowl attached to leather earpieces and held in place by a buckle beneath the chin.

Goggles, now as rare as a carburetor, were necessities against the wind and bugs and particles. When 1949 Indianapolis winner Bill Holland wore racing gloves during a race in the South, some people ridiculed him. Auto racing was no place for frills.

A race driver's attire generally had but one safety device, the primitive helmet. Otherwise his outfit often featured a dirty T-shirt, a pair of his oldest pants, and a well-worn pair of work shoes. For a number of years a Hollywood movie star was brought in to kiss the winner in Victory Lane. She was greeted by a sweat-stained driver speckled with grease and almost certain to embrace her pristine dress with oily hands.

Sometime in the 1950s drivers began wearing coveralls in the race, a habit that eventually would allow dozens of sponsors' logos to be displayed. The coveralls weren't fire retardant and were about the same as those worn by the Texaco Man when he pumped your gas.

A major improvement was made when the cereal bowl helmet evolved into a device that not only absorbed heavier shocks but wrapped down over the ears and lower parts of the head. While still strapped to the chin, this helmet offered wider and better protection than its predecessors. Within a few years these devices were further improved as full-faced helmets were developed.

These advanced helmets are much the same as those used by motorcyclists. Modern racing helmets have an outer shell of carbon fiber, an inner shell of thick polystyrene, and padding that rests against the driver's skull. The tighter the helmet fits, the more protection it offers.[1]

Different brands of helmets offer a smaller opening for seeing than do motorcycle helmets. The view through some racing helmets is barely larger than the size of reading glasses. The strength of some modern helmets is sufficient to turn away a bullet.

Open-cockpit racing has always allowed fans to see the drivers, although this decreased as safety improved. From the beginning the drivers sat high in their seats, leaving their shirts to flop in the wind. Before the helmet size expanded, a few fans seated near the track could recognize the drivers' faces as they passed.

As racing safety improved, the drivers became less visible. By the late 1960s their seats were lower in the cars, which had increased their speed so much it was hard to see the numbers, let alone the drivers.

One way to identify the drivers came through their helmets, which were covered in all types of designs and colors. Usually the helmets were color coded to match the car colors.

Studies have been conducted concerning the effects of head trauma from racing injuries. One study showed that head trauma occurred in 25 percent of racing accidents, which is higher than in any other major international sport. Also, the length of hospital stays for race drivers was the highest. An Australian study also claims motor racing has the highest rate of actual injury among major sports. However, a study made between 1996 and 2000 by Fuji Toranomon Orthopedics Hospital in Shizuoka suggests that only a small portion of these injuries are to the head or surrounding areas.[2]

The prices of racing helmets vary greatly, and the item is not one where drivers or car owners tend to cut corners. One site listed a Bell helmet at about $400. The ad claims it is perfect for drivers who need a wide opening or wear glasses.

Simpson, which has competed with Bell for top-of-the-line products, has one helmet listed at over $600.

The Bell Corporation, based in California, began making polystyrene open-faced helmets in the1950s for racing and law enforcement. Dan Gurney was the first to wear a full faced helmet at Indianapolis, in 1968. The full-faced edition was slower to catch on in NASCAR, where the open-faced version remained popular. Only after Dale Earnhardt was killed at Daytona in 2001 did NASCAR make the full-face type mandatory.

Geoff Bodine was the first NASCAR driver to go to the full-face. NASCAR also required over-the-wall pit crew members to wear helmets, after an accident on pit road caused several head injuries.[3]

21

Keller in Vukovich Crash

ALVAH A. KELLER WAS YOUR PROTOTYPICAL RACING DRIVER OF HIS era. Born in 1920, the Nevada native participated in the top levels of racing between 1949 and 1960. As a champ car driver he won no championships, posted no single-race wins, and won no pole positions. Yet, Al Keller is recalled by most champ car fans of the '50s because of his involvement in one of racing's most remembered accidents.

Keller was first known as a NASCAR driver from 1949 to 1956, when he made 29 career starts, with two victories in 1954. A footnote to his career was being the first to win in stock car racing's top division in a foreign-built car. Keller captured the 1954 Grand National road race in New Jersey in a Jaguar.[1]

On converting to the Indy-type cars, Keller was a rookie in the 500 in 1955. Keller started the race from the 22nd position but spun on the backstretch on the 54th lap. Rodger Ward, who later would win two 500s, spun because of a broken axle and turned over as Keller and Johnny Boyd came up fast.

Keller swerved to avoid Ward and struck Boyd's racer. Boyd skidded between Ward's overturned car and the outer wall. Two-time defending champion Bill Vukovich came along with nowhere to go. The 36-year old Vuky drove over the top of Boyd's racer, cleared the wall, and began a series of flips outside the track. When he landed upside down, the car caught fire with Vukovich trapped inside.

Keller jumped out of his car and ran across the track to help Speedway personnel turn Boyd's car back on its wheels. Boyd suffered only minor injuries from the car skidding on his back.

"Bill's death hit me hard, and I was hurt when a lot of people blamed me," Ward said years later. "But there was nothing I could do."[2]

Investigators said Vukovich had died before the car caught fire.[3]

Vukovich drove in the 500 only five times. Besides winning in 1953 and 1954, he was leading in 1952 when a minor part on his Fuel Injection Special broke and sidelined him with nine laps remaining. He had approximately a half-mile lead at the time he was killed.

During the early moments of the accident Keller sat in his somewhat obsolete dirt car frantically waving his arms to warn oncoming drivers.

In 1961 he qualified 26th fastest for the 500 and came in fifth. Six months later he went to Phoenix, Arizona, to compete on a one-mile dirt track. During the 100-mile race he was involved in a crash that cost him his life.

Keller had started the 1958 race at Indianapolis in 29th position and finished 11th. He was on Ward's pit crew in the 1960 race.

22

Thomson Known for Bravery

LIKE NEW YORK GIANTS HERO BOBBY THOMSON, RACE DRIVER JOHNNY Thomson was nicknamed the Flying Scot. The handle probably better fit the driver.

That wasn't the only description of Johnny Thomson. A. J. Foyt, never one to mince words, called him a "big-balled driver." In other words, Thomson was brave and aggressive and was, in racing language, a "charger."

Thomson arrived at the Speedway in 1953 as a 32-year-old veteran of the midget car circuits. The native of Lowell, Massachusetts, had won the 1948 UCOA (United Car Owners Association) New England title by capturing 32 midget races. He would repeat his championship win in 1950 and added the AAA Eastern Division midget championship in 1952.

Thomson arrived as a rookie at Indianapolis in 1953 and made the 33-car starting grid as the last car in the field. From the back row he drove only six laps before an ignition failure sidelined him with a 32nd-place finish. The next year he went 165 laps before his car stalled. In the 1958 race Thomson started 20th and finished 23rd, his car sidelined by a steering problem on lap 52.

Thomson's hard luck ended in 1959 when he won the pole at a speed of 145.906 mph and came in third. The following year he finished fifth.

From 1953 to 1960 Johnny made 69 starts in champ car races, with seven victories and 43 top 10s. Thomson was the first to win a 100-mile dirt track race in less than an hour, that coming at the perilous one-mile circuit in Langhorne, Pennsylvania. Thomson averaged 100.174 mph.[1]

Thomson also excelled in sprint car races, capturing the 1958 US Auto Club's championship. However, a sprint car became Thomson's undoing in 1960, when he was killed at the Great Allentown Fair in Pennsylvania. His car crashed through a fence and flipped into the infield. He was 38.[2]

23

Among All Else, Foyt Is Survivor

ANTHONY JOSEPH FOYT JR. IS ARGUABLY THE GREATEST AMERICAN RACE driver ever. He is also one of the luckiest. Now 83 years old and still an active car owner, Foyt has stared down the Grim Reaper countless times since he was a 23-year-old rookie at the 1958 Indianapolis 500.

Foyt didn't arrive at Indy unannounced, having posted three top-10 finishes as a US Auto Club rookie in 1957. He began racing midgets at age 18 in his father's car. On arriving at the Speedway he was befriended by veteran Pat O'Connor, whose advice was absorbed by the rookie. Having qualified 12th, A. J. started the race from the fourth row.

In no time flat the track in front of him was cluttered with wreckage. A. J. managed to drive through it unscathed, but on his next circuit he saw that the wreckage included O'Connor's burning car. Everything was black, he wrote in his autobiography, *A.J.* On seeing O'Connor's arm sticking up, A. J. questioned if he was tough enough to be a race driver.

Foyt drove every type of racing machine and drove them well, but even great drivers have close calls. A. J.'s closest brush with death probably occurred at Road America, in Elkhart Lake, Wisconsin, in 1990.

Foyt was attempting to make a 90-degree turn at the end of a long straightaway when his brake pedal broke. Foyt's car sailed over a gravel area devised to slow sliding racers and went down a hill into a dirt area.

"I remember a big tree and that guard rail," Foyt said. "I said, 'Ain't no way I can make the corner to the right because it's about a 60 mile an hour corner and I was going close to 200.'

"When it went off I seen them treetops and I said, 'Man, this ain't going to be one of them I'm going to get out and wave to the crowd. It's going to be rough, and it was rough."

Foyt said he missed hitting a boulder by about five feet, which probably would have proved fatal. He said his pain was so intense that he seriously asked rescuers to knock him out by hitting him in the head with a hammer.

Years later he visited Road America and said, "The hurtin' started all over again."[1]

Foyt was dueling with Dominic Dobson entering the turn.

"I was going to tuck in behind him and follow his line," Dobson said, "but his line was straight. It looked like he never even tried to brake."[2]

Foyt adjusted to the changing conditions of racing over almost four decades. As an Indy rookie in 1958, he qualified at 143.130 mph. He ran his final race at Indy in 1992 with a qualifying speed of 222.799. He drove all types of cars in the 500, won seven Cup races in stock cars, and adjusted to the most modern machines as an Indy car owner.

"He has forgotten more things about racing than I know," former 500 winner Danny Sullivan said.

No one has been more supportive of the Indianapolis 500 than Foyt, who won in 1961, 1964, 1967, and 1977.

"Lots of people say I helped make the Indy 500 as popular as it is, and I don't think that's true," he told *Autoweek* magazine. "A. J. Foyt didn't make the Indy 500, the Indy 500 made A. J. Foyt. I believe that in my heart.

"I've won a lot of places, but if I hadn't won Indy I wouldn't have [been as well known]. Indy was my whole life, still is."[3]

Foyt won his final Indy car race at Pocono Raceway in Long Pond, Pennsylvania, in 1981. It was a record ninth victory in a 500-mile event.

Foyt won a record 67 champ car races and seven national IndyCar Series titles.

24

Sachs Almost Won in '61

EDDIE SACHS WAS A SECOND-YEAR DRIVER IN THE 1958 INDY 500, HAVING finished 23rd the prior year. He led one lap in the '58 race, but his car had transmission problems on the 68th lap and he finished 22nd.

Eddie had a dynamic personality that resonated with the fans. Nicknamed the Clown Prince of Auto Racing, the Pennsylvania native was an entertainer in racing gear. Once after falling out of the race he rolled a tire down the track to thundering applause. Another time after a mishap he coined the phrase, "If you can't win, be spectacular."

Eddie was no clown behind the wheel, although his chief mechanic, Clint Brawner, said he knew little about the car itself. He wasn't a driver who could relate to his crew how a car was handling, but he did know how to go fast.[1]

Sachs started the 1959 race in the middle of the front row but finished 17th after encountering mechanical problems with 18 laps to go. He started the 1960 and 1961 races on the pole, giving him three straight races in which he posted no worse than the second-best qualifying speed.

Tony Bettenhausen had been favored to win the pole in 1961 but was killed the day before time trials began. The magic 150-mph lap appeared to be in reach for Bettenhausen, but Sachs's pole-winning speed of 147.481 fell short, to be broken by Parnelli Jones in 1962.

Jim Hurtubise, who barely missed the 150-mph lap in 1960, jumped ahead of front-row rivals Sachs and Don Branson to lead the first 35 laps of the race. Jim

Rathmann and Jones, a rookie, each had brief stints at the front before Sachs returned to lead for six laps.

Jones, A. J. Foyt, and former winner Troy Ruttman took turns in front before Foyt and Sachs swapped the top spot through 400 miles. With 32 laps remaining, it was a two-car race.

Foyt pitted on the 184th lap after he had failed to get sufficient fuel on a prior stop. That gave the lead to Sachs, who was ahead by a substantial 25 seconds.

Stunningly, Sachs suddenly pulled into the pits with three laps remaining. One of his car's rear tires was showing heavy tread wear, and Sachs decided it was too risky to continue. Foyt took the lead and won his first 500 by 8.3 seconds.

Countless racing people, including Brawner, wondered if Sachs had overreacted and should have tried to finish the race.[2]

Even as racing fans were mourning Bettenhausen, another fatality occurred at the Speedway. During the race Eddie Johnson spun in the fourth turn but wasn't injured. John Masariu, 38, a father of six who was working on the fire-safety crew, was killed when he either fell or jumped from a fire truck that then backed over him. Masariu was the principal of Ben Davis Junior High School in Indianapolis.

25

The Little Car That Could

A. J. FOYT WINNING THE 1961 INDIANAPOLIS 500 WASN'T THE BIGGEST story of the day. The biggest story was the ninth-place finish of Australian Jack Brabham.

Brabham, a two-time Formula One world champion, qualified for the race as the 17th fastest at 145.144 mph. He drove a rear-engine car called the Cooper Climax that would change the face of auto racing in America.

The Cooper Climax was a low-slung British vehicle unlike any of the American cars. It was the first significant rear-engine car at the Speedway since before World War II. The car was significantly slower in the straightaways than the more powerful roadsters that had dominated the 500 since the mid-1950s.

Brabham's strategy was to run the 500 miles with only two pit stops, so he drove at a conservative pace that saw him uncompetitive on the straights but faster through the track's four turns. As things evolved, Brabham still had to make three pit stops, and some believe if he had run a more aggressive race he might have contended for the win.

Brabham led what would become known as the "British invasion," in which a bevy of European drivers and cars would cross the ocean to compete at Indianapolis. Brabham would be followed by Jim Clark, Jackie Stewart, Graham Hill, and Jochen Rindt as foreign drivers converged upon the Speedway

American drivers were tormented by the decision to drive their familiar roadsters or the rear-engine machines. The roadsters were more powerful but didn't handle as well as their rear-engine rivals. Drivers acknowledged that the latter could go farther into the turns before braking, yet some felt uncomfortable in them.

Until the 1950s most cars in the Indianapolis 500 were the same as those used on dirt tracks. The roadster was a sleeker car with an offset engine. The driver sat on the right side of the car with the drive shaft on his left, creating better handling than its predecessor. The dirt track car didn't win at Indy after Troy Ruttman's victory in 1952.

Ruttman's win came after Bill Vukovich's Fuel Injection Special went out with nine laps remaining. But the Fuel Injection Special dominated the 1953 and 1954 races. Also in 1952, the Cummins Diesel Special won the pole at Indy with popular Freddie Agabashian driving.

The newfangled Indy cars made a big stride in 1963, when Clark was runner-up to Parnelli Jones in the 500 and Dan Gurney came in seventh. While Jones won the race in Calhoun, one of the Speedway's legendary roadsters, much of the sentimentality was directed at the Lotus-Fords, driven by Clark and Gurney and prepared by Britain's Colin Chapman.

Jones started on the pole and with 59 laps to go had a 43-second lead over second-place Clark. Eddie Sachs spun twice in the waning laps, the second spin creating a controversy about oil on the track.

"I spun in Parnelli Jones's oil," Sachs insisted.

Jones's car was trailing smoke and seemingly leaking oil. However, car owner J .C. Agajanian convinced officials the leak had ceased because the oil now was below the level of the crack. Officials decided against bringing Jones in for consultation.

Sachs and Jones got into a scuffle the day after the race while arguing about the oil issue.[1]

26

Everyone Loved the Novi

POSSIBLY THE MOST POPULAR RACE CAR EVER TO CIRCLE THE INDI-
anapolis Motor Speedway was the Novi, an extremely loud and powerful vehicle that appeared capable of winning the 500 but had a star-crossed existence.

Behind the car's popularity was the noisy supercharged V8 engine. In the
early years many fans' only connection with the 500-mile race was the Indianapolis Motor Speedway Radio Network, which consisted largely of the
sounds of race cars going past the microphone. The Novi had a penetrating
wailing sound that was easily recognizable.

Many racing people believe the popularity of the sport revolves around the
sound of the cars. Andy Granatelli, a force behind the Novis, brought turbine
cars to the Speedway in 1967 and 1968. Boasting jet-type engines, the cars lacked
engine noise and, despite almost winning the race both years, were legislated
out of the sport.

The Novi Special goes back to 1941, when a car was built with 450 horsepower but was difficult to handle. It was named the Winfield. After the war it
returned as the Novi with 510 horsepower and front-wheel drive. The primary
driver of the Novi for several years was the popular Duke Nalon, and in 1949
Nalon and Rex Mays placed Novis in the first two spots of the field.[1]

Car owner Lew Welch was so confident his Novis would dominate the field
that he told Nalon and Mays on race morning that whoever led the first lap
should be allowed to lead the race. According to George Peters, author of the

book *Novi: The Legendary Indianapolis Race Car,* Welch didn't want the two powerful cars racing each other. He said if the cars finished one-two the winnings would be split evenly between Nalon and Mays.

While leading that race Nalon was involved in one of the most spectacular crashes in Speedway history. His Novi's rear axle shaft broke and his car hit the wall in the north chute and caught fire. Flames crossed the track and ran along the outer wall. Several drivers, including eventual winner Bill Holland, had to drive through the flames.

The Novi's inability to finish races, and its role in the practice session deaths of drivers Ralph Hepburn and Chet Miller, painted a jinx label on the car.

"They were jinxed. You get to believing in the jinx when they happen to you," Nalon said prior to his death in 2001.[2]

Until 1956 the Novis were low-slung vehicles easily identified as they passed the grandstand. In '56 the Novi team changed the looks of the cars and made them rear-wheel-drive vehicles. Paul Russo was named to drive the still powerful entry, and the large number of Novi fans looked forward to success.

During the early laps of the 1956 race Russo moved his fire-engine-red Novi into the lead and held it for 21 laps until a tire blew and threw him into the first-turn wall.

The last Novi appeared at the Speedway in 1966 but failed to make the race. Two Novis were in the 1958 Indy field, with Bill Cheesbourg starting in the last row and finishing 10th. Russo qualified 14th and came in 18th.

27

Innocent Victims

PERHAPS THE MOST INNOCENT VICTIM OF MOTOR RACING WAS WILBUR Brink, whose parents lived on Georgetown Road at the west side of the Indianapolis Motor Speedway in 1932.

Wilbur was 12 years old and went into his front yard to play, oblivious to the Indianapolis 500 auto racing except for the loud noises coming across the Speedway fence.

Defending champion Billy Arnold was leading in the race on the 162nd lap when the rear axle of his race car broke near the fourth turn. One of the wheels sailed high over the fence, crossed Georgetown Road, and struck an innocent Wilbur Brink in his front yard.

Although most of them feel safe, fans who attend auto races must know there is a chance of injury. Many keep that in mind when they select a seat location for an auto race. Such was the case when Lyle Kurtenbach bought a ticket for the 1987 Indianapolis 500 and was sitting in the top row of a grandstand on the north end of the 2.5-mile track.

On the 130th lap a wheel came off Tony Bettenhausen's car and was struck by the nose of Roberto Guerrero's racer. Like a kicked football, the loose tire flew high into the stands and killed Kurtenbach.[1]

Guerrero, unaware of the fatality, assumed he had avoided a serious accident and said, "We were so lucky."

Michael Terry, Sheryl Ann Laster, and Kenneth Dale Fox probably felt safe when they went to the US 500 at Michigan International Speedway in 1998. On the 176th lap of the 250-lap race, driver Adrian Fernandez lost control of his car and slid into a wall at more than 200 miles an hour. The accident displaced the right front wheel, and it soared over a 4-foot wall and an 11-foot fence into the grandstand.

Three were killed, and six other spectators were hospitalized with injuries.[2]

A similar tragedy occurred at Lowe's Motor Speedway in Charlotte, North Carolina, in 1999 when a wreck involving three Indy cars sent debris into the stands and injured nine people.[3] The cars of John Paul Jr. and Stan Wattles hit the fourth-turn wall and went spinning down the front stretch, collecting the car of Scott Harrington.[4]

Indy car drivers depend on their cars collapsing during an accident, which takes much of the blunt trauma from the collision. This can be more dangerous for spectators because of flying debris.

One safety measure adopted after these accidents was to install tethers on the wheels of the cars so they cannot fly away.

28

Sport Loses Two Good Men

COMING INTO THE 1964 INDIANAPOLIS 500, ANTICIPATION WAS AT A fever pitch for several reasons. First, the invasion of foreign drivers was growing, and many red-blooded Americans were bent on seeing the host nation dominate the race. A. J. Foyt and Parnelli Jones were the best bets among the Americans, and Rodger Ward, Bobby Marshman, Lloyd Ruby, Jim Hurtubise, Dan Gurney, and Eddie Sachs all had the credentials to win.

On the European side, Jim Clark was coming off a second-place finish, Jack Brabham had introduced a newfangled race car three years earlier, and such Formula One stars as Jackie Stewart, Graham Hill, and Jochen Rindt were on the verge of entering cars at Indianapolis.

With the British invasion came the added arrival of the rear-engine car first introduced by Brabham in 1961. Most drivers tested both the standard roadster and the rear-engine machines. Most preferred the handling of the latter and changed. Some, such as Jones, Foyt, and Hurtubise, opted to stay with the roadster.

One, rookie Dave MacDonald, had reservations about his rear-engine streamlined vehicle designed by Mickey Thompson. MacDonald had an outstanding record driving sports cars and stock cars but didn't like the handling of his Indy car. His father urged him to back out of his contract with Thompson.[1]

The opening day of qualifying saw Clark win the pole. Before the day ended Ward had set a new track record and Marshman increased it to 157.867 mph.

The record fell again when Clark qualified his Lotus at 159.337. The first 150-mph speed had occurred only two years earlier.[2]

As was traditional at the time, filling the field required four days of time trials, and during that time MacDonald's car continued its poor handling. One conflicting report had Clark advising MacDonald to get out of the car.[3] Nonetheless, the rookie qualified it without incident and would start the race from the middle of the 10th row.

Race day began with sunshine and optimism. As the vast crowd settled into its seats, the Purdue University band played the national anthem and Vic Damone sang "Back Home Again in Indiana." Speedway president Tony Hulman gave the command, "Gentlemen, Start Your Engines" and Benson Ford pulled away in the Ford Mustang pace car.

Everything was in order when the green flag dropped and Clark pulled away to a sizeable lead. Anxiety tugs at every heartstring when the 33-car field approaches the first turn, but in 1964 the field pulled through it cleanly. Fast-beating hearts calmed slightly at the end of the first lap.

Whatever reservations MacDonald had about his car were laid aside during the first lap when he passed five cars. The California driver had the reputation as a "charger," one who aggressively attempts to move up instead of driving conservatively.[4]

Coming out of the fourth turn on the second lap MacDonald's car spun and hit the inside wall, rupturing the fuel tank and igniting the gasoline within. MacDonald's car then slid back across the track as seven other cars became involved. Ronnie Duman was burned when his car spun amid the flames and crashed into the inside wall. Bobby Unser, driving a Novi, struck Johnny Rutherford's car and crashed into the outside wall. Chuck Stevenson and Norm Hall also crashed as a vast cloud of black smoke arose over the straightaway, drifting toward the nearby spectators.

Unser and Rutherford both were second-year drivers and would go on to win six 500s between them.

Rutherford said the fact that he was driving a roadster instead of a rear-engine car probably saved his life. "If I'd been in the rear-engine car it would have broken apart and stopped in the middle of the fire," he said.

Sachs tried to get through the wreck by aiming for a spot near the outside wall, only to strike MacDonald's sliding car broadside. That caused a second explosion, and the crash killed Sachs instantly. Although Sachs was trapped in his car there were only modest burns to his face and hands. A tarp was placed over his car and it was towed away.

Sachs was known to put a lemon on a string and put it around his neck so he could suck on the fruit during the race. After the wreckage was cleared, the lemon was found in Rutherford's car.[5]

MacDonald, although badly burned, was still alive and was taken to the infield hospital. He died some four hours later at Methodist Hospital.

Bill Marvel, longtime public relations official at the track, recalled an ominous conversation he had had with Sachs.

"I will never forget this. In 1964 he stopped by the press room on Sunday evening. He had just qualified; he had crashed on Saturday and had to qualify on Sunday," Marvel recalled. "He was hanging out in the press room and we were just getting ready to close up and Eddie came by.

"I said, 'Well, you finally got in the race today,' and he said, 'Yeah, I'll tell you. I sure hate to start behind MacDonald.' We didn't get into the conversation any further," Marvel said. "MacDonald hadn't driven on ovals much, if any at all. He was a road racer."

Marvel said he had another encounter with Sachs later that night that gave insight into Eddie's character.

"The night before the race that year I'm coming out of the Holiday Inn across the street," Marvel said. "He sees me and says, 'What are you guys doing?' And, I said, 'I'm trying to sell a couple of extra tickets I've got.' He got up on a chair and started trying to get people to come up and buy those from me."

The race was stopped for the first time in history. On resuming, Clark led four more laps before Bobby Marshman moved into first place for 32 laps.[6] Marshman was one of the rising stars of the sport, but the following November 27 he was conducting tire tests at the one-mile track in Phoenix, Arizona, and crashed into the wall, rupturing the fuel tank.[7] Marshman wasn't wearing fire-retardant clothing and six days later died of burns.[8]

Foyt went on to win his second 500, with Ward second.

Sachs had married Nance McGarrity in 1959 and had a son, Eddie III, who tried racing for a time but never got to the 500. Later remarried, Nance continued to follow racing until her death in 2005, at which time she was buried beside Eddie 41 years after his death.

MacDonald's wife, Sherry, had no desire to remain close to the sport that had cost her a husband. But before the 100th Indy 500 in 2016 she returned to the Speedway. A picture was taken of her there with her son, Rich, and Eddie Sachs III.[9]

29

He Was a Wonderful Gentleman

THE POPULARITY OF THE INDIANAPOLIS 500 INCREASED AFTER THE race was broadcast "flag to flag" beginning in 1952 when the IMS Radio Network was founded. Although some radio coverage of the race dates back to the 1920s, the network stepped up its coverage and made Sid Collins a household name among fans.

From 1952 to 1985 the IMS Radio Network was the only outlet with live coverage of the race, and the golden-voiced Collins was the centerpiece of the broadcast. With the exception of the 1949 and 1950 races, which were shown locally, live home television coverage didn't occur until 1986. Collins and his team of announcers around the track kept listeners informed about action in the race. Their biggest nightmare was an accident, such as the one in 1964.

Collins, who worked for Indianapolis station WIBC, was the chief announcer from 1952 to 1977. His impromptu eulogy of Eddie Sachs during the 1964 race was his most famous work. The network received more than 30,000 letters asking for a copy of the on-air eulogy.[1]

Speedway public address announcer Tom Carnegie had announced the death of Sachs (MacDonald was still alive at the time), and the radio broadcast carried Carnegie's words. The radio broadcast was silent for a time before Collins began a solemn, impromptu eulogy:

You heard the announcement from the public address system. There's not a sound. Men are taking off their hats. People are weeping. There are over 300,000 fans here not moving. Disbelieving.

Some men try to conquer life in a number of ways. These days of our outer space attempts some men try to conquer the universe. Race drivers are courageous men who try to conquer life and death and they calculate their risks. And with our talking with them over the years I think we know their inner thoughts in regards to racing. They take it as part of living.

A race driver who leaves this earth mentally when he straps himself into the cockpit to try what for him is the biggest conquest he can make (are) aware of the odds and Eddie Sachs played the odds. He was serious and frivolous. He was fun. He was a wonderful gentleman. He took much needling and he gave much needling. Just as the astronauts do perhaps.

These boys on the racetrack ask no quarter and they give none. If they succeed, they're a hero, and if they fail, they tried. And it was Eddie's desire and will to try with everything he had, which he always did. So the only healthy way perhaps we can approach the tragedy of the loss of a friend like Eddie Sachs is to know that he would have wanted us to face it as he did. As as [sic] it has happened, not as we wish it would have happened. It is God's will, I'm sure, and we must accept that.

We are all speeding toward death at the rate of 60 minutes every hour, the only difference is, we don't know how to speed faster, and Eddie Sachs did. So since death has a thousand or more doors, Eddie Sachs exits this earth in a race car. Knowing Eddie, I assume that's the way he would have wanted it. Byron said "who the Gods love, die young."

Eddie was 37. To his widow Nancy we extend our extreme sympathy and regret. And to his two children. This boy won the pole here in 1961 and 1962 [sic]. He was a proud race driver. Well, as we do at Indianapolis and in racing, as the World Champion Jimmy Clark I'm sure would agree as he's raced all over the world, the race continues. Unfortunately today, without Eddie Sachs. And we'll be restarting it in just a few moments.[2]

Collins committed suicide in 1977 after learning he had ALS, Lou Gehrig's disease.

30

Fire and Fear Are Synonymous

FIRE HAD BECOME A CONCERN IN AUTO RACING EVEN BEFORE THE inferno at Indianapolis in 1964 claimed two lives. A. J. Foyt said fire was the race driver's biggest fear, and when popular Jim Hurtubise was severely burned shortly after the Sachs-MacDonald tragedy, the sport looked harder for safety measures.

Hurtubise became an instant hero when he came within a few thousands of a second of doing the first 150-mph lap at the Speedway. It occurred on the final day of qualifying in 1960 when Hurtubise was a rookie.

Hurtubise's crash at Milwaukee resulted in serious burns that curtailed but didn't end his career. His hands were severely burned, and doctors said they would have to be given a permanent shape. Hurtubise could choose if he wanted the fingers straight or bent.

"Just make 'em so I can hold a steering wheel," he said.[1]

Herk, as everyone called him, started his career in NASCAR and won one race in 36 attempts. He never finished higher than 13th in the 500. He was at the track 21 years but failed to qualify 11 times. His Mallard was the last roadster to appear at the Speedway, but it never was competitive.

On "bump day" in 1972 his crew put his car in line for a qualification attempt. The deadline for qualifying passed before his time came to take out the Miller beer-sponsored vehicle. Hurtubise then removed the car's engine cover to show that the car had no engine and was filled with his sponsor's beer, which he generously shared.

Hurtubise died on January 6, 1989, at age 56.

A fire in the pits at the 1981 Indy 500 resulted in Rick Mears receiving serious burns. During his stop, fuel began pouring from a refueling hose before it was connected to the car. The fuel was methanol, which burns with no visible flame or smoke, and Mears was on fire from the waist up. He leaped from the car and ran to the pit wall where a safety worker, seeing no flame, tried to remove his helmet. Mears finally leaped over the pit wall, but the fire wasn't extinguished until his father, Bill, realized the dilemma and sprayed him. Mears and four members of his crew were sent to the hospital, and Mears later had plastic surgery on his face.[2]

The danger of fire was not limited to Indy cars. Glenn "Fireball" Roberts was a major star in NASCAR whose catchy nickname was not a product of his racing but of his outstanding fast ball as a pitcher.

At the World 600 in 1964 he was involved in a crash with Ned Jarrett and Junior Johnson. Roberts's car landed on its roof and gasoline spilled throughout the driver's area. Jarrett pulled him out of the car, but Fireball had burns over 80 percent of his body. He died weeks later.

Roberts once was pulled over by a traffic cop, who said, "Who do you think you are, Fireball Roberts?"

"Yes, yes, I do," he responded.[3]

Fiery accidents also left deep wounds in Formula One, the world's most touted racing circuit. The 1967 Monaco Grand Prix, famous for its path through the winding streets of Monte Carlo, saw Italian driver Lorenzo Bandini lose his life in a horrible fiery crash. Ronnie Peterson was killed in a like crash at the start of the 1978 Italian Grand Prix at Monza. Peterson was a teammate of American Mario Andretti, who clinched the world championship in the race.

Those who meet Niki Lauda will recognize that fire has crossed his path. The Austrian race driver owns three world championships but was burned badly in the 1976 German Grand Prix.[4]

Perhaps the most notable element in the Sachs-MacDonald crash was the fuel being used in the rear-engine cars. The traditional fuel used in Indy cars was methanol. Cars in 1964 housed the fuel in a metal tank that could rupture and spill fuel onto hot surfaces.

The solution was to develop a rubber bladder that fitted inside the tank and didn't rupture.

Another improvement was the development of fire-retardant uniforms, Numerous drivers avoided major burns because these uniforms gave them a certain amount of time and protection from the blaze.

Auto racing was especially dangerous in the early years of the Indianapolis Motor Speedway. This photo shows the start of the 1916 race when riding mechanics accompanied drivers in the vehicles. Their job was to watch for cars approaching from behind and to observe the oil pressure. Between the opening of the track in 1909 and 1915 there were nine deaths, including that of two spectators. Indiana Historical Society, P0569; Bass Photo Co. Collection, Indiana Historical Society; Bretzman Collection, Indiana Historical Society.

Speeds at the Speedway have increased from about 75 miles an hour in 1911 to more than a hundred miles per hour faster. The 2.5-mile-long track, shown in the early days, is the same dimension as when Ray Harroun won the initial race. Indiana Historical Society, P0569; Bass Photo Co. Collection, Indiana Historical Society; Bretzman Collection, Indiana Historical Society.

Movie actor Clark Gable sits in the lower left of this picture watching the start of the 1947 Indianapolis race. Mauri Rose and Bill Holland finished one-two as teammates in the dominant Blue Crown Spark Plug Specials. Indiana Historical Society, P0569; Bass Photo Co. Collection, Indiana Historical Society; Bretzman Collection, Indiana Historical Society.

Chet Miller sits in the cockpit of the Novi Pure Lube Special in the early 1950s. The powerful, loud Novi was one of the most popular cars ever driven at the Speedway. Extremely powerful, yet unreliable, the Novi never won at Indianapolis. Miller was killed in a first-turn crash in 1953. Indiana Historical Society, P0569; Bass Photo Co. Collection, Indiana Historical Society; Bretzman Collection, Indiana Historical Society.

The pace car speeds down pit lane at the start of the 1916 race. Before the 1957 race a median was installed between the reconfigured pit lane and the racing surface. The change, which involved cars starting from the pits instead of being parked on the track, caused a confused start each of the two races in which it was used. Indiana Historical Society, P0569; Bass Photo Co. Collection, Indiana Historical Society; Bretzman Collection, Indiana Historical Society.

Race cars slide throughout the third turn and the infield during the first lap of the 1958 Indianapolis 500. Fifteen cars were involved, and eight of them were unable to continue the race. Pat O'Connor, starting from the middle of the second row, was killed when his car flipped over another one and caught fire. Indiana Historical Society, P0569; Bass Photo Co. Collection, Indiana Historical Society; Bretzman Collection, Indiana Historical Society.

The lengthy main straightaway of the Indianapolis Motor Speedway stretches from the first turn back to the fourth. The first corner represents the drivers' most serious challenge, with 33 cars barreling into the corner at the start of the race. Indiana Historical Society, P0569; Bass Photo Co. Collection, Indiana Historical Society; Bretzman Collection, Indiana Historical Society.

A. J. Foyt was a 23-year-old rookie in the 1958 Indianapolis 500, driving the Dean Van Lines Special for mechanic Clint Brawner. Foyt avoided the 15-car accident on the first lap and went on to finish 16th. The Houston, Texas, native went on to win the 500 in 1961, 1964, 1967, and 1977. He continued to compete at Indianapolis through 1993. Courtesy of the Indianapolis Motor Speedway Photo Archive.

Facing, Chief steward Harlan Fengler pulls the three stripes of rookie tape off the car of Paul Goldsmith (left) as mechanic Smokey Yunick looks on. Drivers were required to carry the marking until passing their driver's test. A former motorcycle racer, Goldsmith had Jerry Unser's car run up his back en route to clearing the third-turn wall. Goldsmith survived a successful racing career and lives in northern Indiana. Courtesy of the Indianapolis Motor Speedway Photo Archive.

North Vernon's Pat O'Connor sits in his Sumar Special only days before losing his life in a first-lap accident in the 1958 Indianapolis 500. The 29-year-old O'Connor started in the middle of the second row, and his car hurdled over Jimmy Reece's vehicle after Ed Elisian triggered a massive accident entering the third turn. O'Connor had been one of the race favorites. Courtesy of the Indianapolis Motor Speedway Photo Archive.

Above, Pat O'Connor smiles at bystanders as he waits to take his 1950s-style roadster out for a spin around the Indianapolis Motor Speedway in 1958. O'Connor, one of the sport's most popular drivers, was competing in his fifth Indy 500. His son, Jeff, who was one year old at the time, and his widow, Analice, still live in North Vernon, Indiana. Courtesy of the Indianapolis Motor Speedway Photo Archive.

Right, George Amick was considered a rising star when he finished second in the 1958 race, after which he was named Rookie of the Year. However, a year later he was killed in a spectacular accident on the last lap of a race at Daytona International Speedway. It remains the only IndyCar race on the high-banked Daytona track. Courtesy of the Indianapolis Motor Speedway Photo Archive.

Facing top, Jimmy Bryan, one of the most successful race drivers of his time, was the winner of the 1958 race. He drove the same car that won the previous year when driven by Sam Hanks. Bryan won three national championships and had three top-five finishes in the Indy 500. He died at age 34 when his car flipped several times in the Puke Hollow section of Langhorne Speedway. Courtesy of the Indianapolis Motor Speedway Photo Archive.

Facing bottom, Chuck Weyant, who finished 24th in the 1958 race, was born in 1923 and is the oldest survivor to have driven in an Indianapolis 500. Weyant, a longtime resident of Springfield, Illinois, carried around a picture of his race car while a soldier during World War II. He competed in four Indianapolis races. Courtesy of the Indianapolis Motor Speedway Photo Archive.

Above, Wrecked race cars are scattered around the third turn of the Indianapolis Motor Speedway following a massive crash on May 30, 1958. A first-lap duel between pole-sitter Dick Rathmann and Ed Elisian saw their cars come together in front of the 33-car field, triggering a 15-car accident that killed Pat O'Connor. O'Connor's death came three years after two-time defending champion Bill Vukovich was killed in the 500. Courtesy of the Indianapolis Motor Speedway Photo Archive.

Confusion marked the start of the 1958 race when the three cars in the front row got ahead of the field and had to circle the track to get into the starting grid. From left to right are Jimmy Reece, Ed Elisian, and Dick Rathmann. Elisian and Rathmann had competed for the top speed in practice and continued their duel at the start of the race. Reece and Elisian later were killed in racing accidents. Courtesy of the Indianapolis Motor Speedway Photo Archive.

Art Bisch is shown in the Ansted-Rotary Special with which Pat O'Connor started in the front row in 1956. Bisch was involved in the O'Connor crash in '58 and finished last. He died barely a month later of injuries suffered in a crash at Lakewood Speedway in Atlanta. Two weeks before his death he won an IndyCar race at the Milwaukee Mile. Courtesy of the Indianapolis Motor Speedway Photo Archive.

Above, Pat O'Connor was among the most popular men in North Vernon, Indiana, as a sign at the city's edge reveals. Courtesy of *North Vernon Plain Dealer and Sun.*

Facing, The grave of race driver Pat O'Connor rests beneath this tombstone in Vernon Cemetery, bordering O'Connor's hometown of North Vernon, Indiana. A number of coins, mostly quarters, rest atop the stone, left by visitors in tribute. Photo by the author.

31

Just Get It Over

WHEN THE 1973 INDY RACE BEGAN, IT HAD BEEN ALMOST A DECADE since the last in-race fatality at Indianapolis. Prayers had been said that the 1964 race would be the last of its kind. They were unanswered prayers.

The race started with the always feared multi-car accident on the first turn of the day. Driver Salt Walther was badly burned, and a memorable picture showed his feet sticking through the front end of the car as it slid. Then the weather turned nasty, and the race was delayed for two and a half days. Rain eventually cut the race to only 332.5 miles, and by that time what was left of the massive crowd was ready to go home anyway.

"After the second day you started thinking, 'What's next?' said driver Johnny Rutherford. 'They could have just as well red-flagged the thing and we would have been happy to have gone on to Milwaukee.'"[1]

Bolt-on wings, introduced in 1972, helped Indy cars attain a large increase in speeds that following year when Bobby Unser's pole speed was 17 miles an hour faster than the one in '72.[2]

When the race restarted, Swede Savage was on his 58th lap when his car crashed and disintegrated around him.

Savage was severely burned, and the horror hadn't ended. Pit crewman Armando Teran was running up the track to see if he could help when he was struck by a fire truck traveling an estimated 60 miles an hour in the opposite direction. Teran died of crushed ribs and a fractured skull.[3]

After an hour delay the race resumed, only to be delayed and then canceled because of rain. Gordon Johncock was declared the winner.

Savage lived 33 days after the accident.

32

Danger Highest on Short Tracks

AN INVESTIGATION BY THE *CHARLOTTE OBSERVER* IN 2014 ESTABLISHED that more than 525 racing fatalities had occurred in the United States over the prior 25 years. And it further showed that two out of every three deaths in US auto racing occurred at short tracks.

Short tracks are the lifeblood of American auto racing. They are on the outskirts of hundreds of towns across the land, hosting Friday or Saturday night racing through the warm months. Some cities, such as Salem and Winchester, Indiana, are best known for their tracks.

Most great drivers started their careers on short tracks, many of them no longer than a quarter of a mile. They may be either dirt or asphalt, but all carry a racing atmosphere with the smell—or is it stench—of oil, gasoline, hot asphalt, and hot dogs cooking. The fans are largely rural, dressed in John Deere hats, Dale Earnhardt or A. J. Foyt T-shirts, and tight jeans that wrap around work shoes or cowboy boots.

Short tracks are found everywhere; there once was one across the street from the Indianapolis Motor Speedway. Anderson Speedway in Indiana is nationally known for the Little 500, a sprint-car race preceding the "real" 500 that features 33 sprint cars on a quarter-mile track.

Often local drivers get the opportunity to race against prominent NASCAR or Indy car drivers, who go to short tracks to help draw crowds or because they simply love to race.

These tracks can be dangerous for several reasons. The overall skill of the local drivers is less than those who race at the top levels. If for no other reason than cost, the cars probably aren't as safe as ones the touted drivers use. A 17-year-old kid probably can't afford as good a helmet as, say, Tony Stewart.

Stewart not only owns a short racetrack but has patronized ones like it for years. In 2014 his car struck and killed 20-year-old Kevin Ward Jr. at a New York track. Ward was standing on the track pointing accusingly toward Stewart's car, which was coming toward him. The two had just had an altercation on the track and Ward's car had struck a wall.

Most safety improvements over the years, such as adding fuel cells within metal tanks and roll bars, have come after tragedies. Ward's death resulted in NASCAR mandating that drivers stay in their cars and not walk on the track to confront other drivers.

The *Charlotte Observer* report said 53 percent of the deaths since 1990 were on short tracks, and added that that had climbed to 70 percent between 1990 and 1993.[1]

33

'58 Drivers Can't Escape Fate

BY RACE DAY OF 1961 EIGHT DRIVERS WHO HAD TAKEN THE GREEN FLAG for the 1958 Indianapolis 500 had died in racing accidents. Leading off the list is Pat O'Connor, followed by Art Bisch, Jimmy Reece, George Amick, Jerry Unser, Ed Elisian, Jimmy Bryan, and Tony Bettenhausen. They represented five champ car driving championships, and the potential of such drivers as O'Connor, Bryan, and Amick was unlimited.

By the tenth anniversary of O'Connor's wreck, a total of 22 open-wheel drivers had paid the ultimate price. Of those, 13 were in the 33-car field for the '58 race.

Shorty Templeman was one of the 13. Templeman competed in the Indy 500 from 1955 to 1962, finishing fourth in 1961. The following year he qualified sixth fastest and came in 11th. In the 1958 Indy race he started 23rd and finished 19th.

Clark "Shorty" Templeman was a native of Pueblo, Colorado, and was most successful driving midget cars. Running in the AAA and US Auto Club champ car circuit, he competed from 1954 to 1962. He made 42 starts in champ cars and finished in the top 10 16 times, including runner-up finishes at DuQuoin, Illinois, and Syracuse, New York.[1]

Templeman specialized in racing midgets and won five Washington State and three Oregon midget state championships. He won three Night Before the 500 midget car races held at the 16th Street Speedway across the street from the home of the 500. He also won the USAC National Midget Series championship in 1956, 1957, and 1958.

The 43-year-old Templeman died following a midget car crash at the Marion (Ohio) Fairgrounds on August 24, 1962.[2]

Shorty was in fact short—barely five feet tall. He was scraping for money by working at an Indianapolis gas station in the early '60s when a car slipped off the jack and mashed his leg. He showed up at the next Indianapolis race limping and sleeping in his station wagon. He raced despite many obstacles.[3]

34

Dodge Loses in Photo Finish

POOR JUDGMENT BY DRIVERS WASN'T LIMITED TO THE RACING SURFACE. In fact, one of the most unusual accidents in Speedway history involved the driver of the pace car.

His name was Eldon Palmer, and he was driving to promote the Dodge Challenger 383–4V, a vehicle he was trying to sell at his Indianapolis car dealership. Palmer had been chosen to drive the pace car, which in later years was assigned to a former race driver.

Palmer prepared for his duty by reportedly setting up an orange flag along the pit lane to show him where to start braking. Passengers were to be Speedway president Tony Hulman, ABC announcer Chris Schenkel, and astronaut John Glenn. Palmer had practiced his run on the eve of the race. Whether the orange flag was in place is subject to debate.[1]

As the race started Palmer pulled into the pits and continued to accelerate, reportedly thinking he was to cross the start-finish line before the field of cars. Reaching 125 mph, Palmer realized he was going too fast and braked hard. The Dodge Challenger swerved and skidded to the end of pit lane where it struck a photographer's stand. The stand collapsed and 29 people were injured. Hulman sustained a sprained ankle.[2]

35

Phrase Almost Prophetic

THE LATE JIM MURRAY IS GENERALLY RECOGNIZED AS THE GREATEST sportswriter of all time. Although a native of Connecticut, he was a columnist at the *Los Angeles Times* from 1961 to 1998.

Murray was a kind-hearted man beloved by his peers. He won a Pulitzer Prize, an unusual accomplishment for a sportswriter. He could turn a phrase so magnificently that other writers kicked themselves for not thinking of it first. Murray's writing often was caustic but usually fair, and that alone kept him from being a poison pen.

Murray once wrote that Oakland outfielder Rickey Henderson had a "strike zone the size of Hitler's heart." He said UCLA basketball coach John Wooden was "so square he was divisible by four."

However, the line that made Murray famous was directed at the Indianapolis 500. "Gentlemen, start your coffins," he wrote.

For several years he was one of auto racing's major critics, but auto racing didn't take the brunt of his wit. For instance:

"Los Angeles is under policed and oversexed."

"Tommy Lasorda is as noisy as a bowling alley."

On Billy Martin: "Some people have a chip on their shoulders. Billy has a lumberyard."

On Sonny Liston versus Cassius Clay: "One hundred and eighty million people will be rooting for a double knockout."[1]

Murray's feelings about the Indianapolis 500 may have mellowed in the years before his death in 1998. He was a fixture in the pressroom in later years and showed no malice toward the race.

36

Later That Night He Was Gone

BILL MARVEL MAY BE INTO RACING AS DEEPLY AS ANYONE. HE HAS BEEN around the Indianapolis Motor Speedway for most of his 78 years. He used to race himself, and both of his sons, Billy and Brad, drove race cars.

Yet, Marvel is more than a fan. He is a victim who paid the ultimate price for loving racing. He also is a man who weighed the losses beforehand and lived with them later.

Billy Marvel became a racing fan because his father's love of the sport rubbed off. On September 17, 1983, Billy was killed in an accident at Lincoln Park Speedway in Putnamville, Indiana. Years later his father summarized his loss and, in some manner, justified it.

"I've had a lot of time to think about this. I don't have regrets about him racing. I wish he was still with us, but when you grow up racing it becomes a powerful love," Marvel told *Sports Illustrated* in 2013. "You accept that it can take everything from you, but you still do it because of that love."[1]

Sports Illustrated estimated there have been 15 auto racing fatalities each year since 2001.

Marvel is executive director of the USAC Benevolent Foundation, which raises money for the families of killed or injured drivers. He responded to a question about racing being addictive with a chuckle.

"Oh, definitely. Yeah. I think it gets in your blood. I don't think anybody ever gets away from it," he said, adding that he never blamed the sport for the loss of his son.

"Oh, no! Not once. Oh, no," he responded. "At the time he got killed I was with USAC. We were having within the state of Indiana what was called the G. C. Murphy Indiana Sprint Car Series," he recalled. "At the funeral the fellow that put everything together was there and I went up to him and said, 'I don't want this to affect your interest in what we're doing in the sprint car series.' I said, 'Billy would not want that to happen.'"

In a similar light, Marvel knows that race car drivers believe tragedy will strike others but "it will never happen to me."

"Don't you think all of us go through life thinking that guy died but I'm not going to?" he answered. "Billy was a fireman. He would have been just as happy to die in a race car."

Bill Marvel drove for a time, buying a car so he could drive in the same events as Billy.

"Billy was driving stock cars, and I bought a stock car from a local guy and I raced it," Bill said. "That was in late 1975. I went over to Dayton, Ohio, and started on the pole of a stock car race. I probably ran about 30 laps and got into a steel guardrail with the right side and wiped out the two tires on that side.

"I drove for a year, and I'm glad I did because Billy and I spent a lot of time together that summer."

Billy Marvel was interviewed by the track announcer before the race in which he was killed. He'd been having trouble with his car, and the announcer referred to this and said, "Billy, you've been having trouble in your rookie year."

According to his father, Billy Marvel said, "That's up to the Lord. Some nights He doesn't want us out here and some nights He does. That's just the way it is."

"Later that night he was gone," Bill said.[2]

37

Jud Larson, A Breed Apart

JUD LARSON WAS THE LAST OF THE 13 DRIVERS IN THE 1958 INDIAN-apolis 500 who died in racing accidents. It occurred on June 11, 1966, in Reading, Pennsylvania, and it also took the life of William (Red) Riegel.

Larson was a rookie in the 1958 Indy 500 and finished in eighth place, eight spots ahead of another rookie, A. J. Foyt. Larson would have been Rookie of the Year most years, but George Amick's second-place finish helped him clinch that honor.

Larson really didn't enjoy racing on anything but dirt. He preferred to power slide through turns and didn't really like brakes. His team actually rigged up a second brake pedal, which they termed the "Oh, Jesus bar," and told Jud it was for use only when he went so deep in the turn that it scared him. The wooden brake pedal was bogus.[1]

Larson raced in only one more Indianapolis race, coming in 29th the following year when he was involved in an accident on the 45th lap. His reputation wasn't built at Indy but on the many dirt tracks across America. Larson drove the US Auto Club's champ cars, in which he made 53 starts and won 7 races. He had 38 top-10 finishes.[2]

Larson, 43, and Riegel, 34, were killed on the second lap of a 30-lap feature. Their cars got together and went up a small embankment. The cars flipped over and trapped the drivers inside. Larson, a Texan, had been racing since he was 16.[3]

Jud had the reputation of a hard-driving, hard-drinking, hard-living dude, and may have been the prototypical race driver of his day. Jim Chini, who followed Larson's career closely, posted an article in a Yahoo! History Group in which he said Larson "could drive anything, anywhere, against anyone, on any surface and, if he were hungry enough, be in contention for the win." Added Chini, "He only held three or four 'real jobs' in his lifetime and those were always short-lived."

38

A New Rival for Indy

PAT O'CONNOR DIDN'T LIVE TO SEE IT HAPPEN, BUT WHEN HE DIED THE biggest changes in American racing history were about to unfold.

In 1958 the Indianapolis 500 was unchallenged as the world's most famous race. The Grand Prix of Monaco may have had more charm, especially with Grace Kelly living there, but a win at Indy followed a driver all his life. Stock car racing was big in the South, but most of NASCAR's stars didn't want any part of open-wheel racing. Richard Petty won 200 stock car races but refused to try Indianapolis.

But with the opening of Daytona International Speedway in 1959, stock cars began moving to the forefront of racing's publicity machine. At first open-wheel racing didn't feel threatened, and stars such as A. J. Foyt and Parnelli Jones still won most of the popularity contests. Indianapolis also got a big boost when some of the Formula One stars decided to try the Speedway, bringing their low-slung mesmerizing race cars with them.

Europeans Jim Clark and Graham Hill won the 500, and Jackie Stewart became a favorite of the American fans. Yet, even as the 500 went through positive years, there were reasons why NASCAR eventually became the country's favorite racing venue.

For one thing, cable television was becoming a staple of the American home and the cable stations were looking for popular sports events to fill their schedule. NASCAR ran more races than champ cars and was popular with

sponsors because there was ample room on the fenders and hood for adver-
tising space.

Indianapolis-style racing used speed as its drawing power. For decades
hundreds of thousands of fans attended time trials, and speed records sometimes were broken two or three times a day. Stock cars, which were substan-
tially slower, didn't advertise speed as much as close racing. Indy cars didn't
run quite as close, because of the danger of faster speeds and the possibility of
wheels touching.

NASCAR further profited from the fact that its race cars looked like pas-
senger cars, even if there were few other similarities. A family driving a Ford
cheered for the Ford drivers; likewise with other models. This competition was
rewarding for car dealers.

"It's no secret that what wins on Sunday sells on Monday," driver Darrell
Waltrip said.[1]

At some point NASCAR began attracting the best young drivers, including Indiana products Jeff Gordon and Tony Stewart. Mostly because there was
more earning potential in NASCAR, some Indy champions such as Sam Hornish Jr. and Dario Franchitti switched to stock cars.

"For a stock-car driver to go to Indianapolis is pretty much like a pro football player signing up with a baseball team," former NASCAR driver Cale Yarborough said in his autobiography, *Cale*.[2]

Perhaps it's inaccurate, but the racing deaths of Bill Vukovich, O'Connor,
Eddie Sachs, and Dave MacDonald left the impression that Indy racing was
more dangerous. Waltrip once addressed that topic when he said, "At Indianapolis there's a quiet hush that comes over the crowd when a driver hits the
wall at 200 mph because they assume the driver's dead. In our sport the driver
gets out and he's hot. The car's torn up and is out of the race. He's stomping
around, kicking and throwing his helmet. At Indianapolis they don't do that."[3]

Still, NASCAR experienced its own dangers, including the death of Glenn
"Fireball" Roberts in 1964. Richard Petty's grandson, Adam, was killed racing. Daytona International Speedway hosted multiple races each year, and the
track experienced 27 fatalities from 1959 to 2001, when Dale Earnhardt was
killed there.

Safety wasn't the only issue troubling the Indianapolis Motor Speedway in
the 1990s. Anton Hulman (Tony) George, grandson of late Speedway owner
Tony Hulman, assumed the presidency of the Speedway. George, born one year

after O'Connor's death, quickly became the most controversial figure in racing.

George's biggest change involved the formation of the Indy Racing League (IRL) in 1994. In doing so he used the Indy 500 as his trump card, which resulted in a split between the top open-wheel factions and a falloff in the popularity of the Greatest Spectacle in Racing.

George founded the IRL for several reasons, including safety. He launched a circuit of all-oval racing; the preceding Championship Auto Racing Teams (CART) had also raced on street and road courses. George wanted to reduce speeds and changed engine modifications to do so. Because the success of foreign drivers had made it more difficult for American drivers to get rides, George wanted the IRL to open doors for them to race at Indianapolis.

CART had the bulk of well-known open-wheel drivers in its stable, but lacked its main attraction in the 500. The first of the IRL-sanctioned 500s was run with no new race cars. The number of tents and motor homes at the 500 was far below its customary number. Many of the normal newspaper reporters weren't sent by their companies. With such popular drivers as Michael Andretti and Al Unser Jr. absent, there was less interest.

CART teams began to race again at Indianapolis in 2000, building new cars to meet IRL specifications. The split continued until 2008 when the two factions merged.

In the meantime, however, many former open-wheel supporters shifted their allegiance to NASCAR, for which George was frequently blamed.

Whatever blame he is assigned about the IRL must be weighed against the positive things he accomplished. One of those involved the way he improved the Speedway's atmosphere since it reopened after the war.

The Speedway infield had the reputation of being an undesirable place to take women and children. Profane messages often covered clothing, which sometimes was sparse anyway. The infield inside the first turn was dubbed the "snake pit" and was the site of all kinds of misadventures. Veteran Speedway visitors used to wonder how many babies had been conceived in the snake pit.

Under Tony George the snake pit was closed. Food service was vastly improved, and once muddy parking lots were covered with asphalt. Flags and giant photos of Speedway heroes decorated the pedestrian areas. A concrete plaza was installed inside the front stands. Concerts brought in big-name singers and bands, and pre-race festivities included an impressive honoring of the military.

A tiny, dirty press room was replaced by a massive facility with many amenities.

George also was behind the building of an infield road circuit, used to lure Formula One into running the US Grand Pix there. He built a control tower that dwarfed its predecessor and installed exit and entry roads to make entering and leaving the pits safer. And while only one race a year was run at the Speedway during his grandfather's tenure, George brought in the Brickyard 400 as a NASCAR event.

The Indianapolis Motor Speedway often is accurately credited with being on the cutting age of safety. Nowhere was that more evident than with the creation of the "SAFER barrier," which can reduce the trauma of hitting a concrete wall up to 50 percent.

With Speedway backing, the SAFER (steel and foam energy reduction) barrier was developed by engineers at the University of Nebraska. In 2002 the Indianapolis Motor Speedway became the first track to install these.

The SAFER barrier consists of sections of steel tubing backed by foam blocks installed 30 inches in front of the traditional wall. The closed cell foam absorbs much of the impact.

George was forced out of his position as CEO of the Speedway by his mother and sisters in 2009.

39

Ward's Time Finally Arrives

FAME CAME SLOWLY FOR RODGER WARD, WHO FINALLY WON HIS FIRST Indy 500 in his ninth year at the Speedway. Ward qualified seventh fastest as a rookie in 1951 but didn't finish higher than eighth in his first six races. His eighth-place finish in 1956 marked the first time he even finished the 500 miles.

"Ward "was one of the greats of all time, [but] it didn't start out that way," said Robin Miller of *Racer* magazine. "Ward's first five or six years he bounced around. He didn't . . . have a great reputation, crashed quite a bit."

Some assign Ward a role in the Bill Vukovich fatality in 1955, when Ward's spin on the backstretch triggered a four-car accident that sent Vuky's car tumbling outside the fence.

Ward's career took off when he joined the Leader Card team in 1959. Headed by owner Bob Wilke and master mechanic A. J. Watson, Leader Card won the '59 race with Ward at the wheel. He qualified in the second row and dominated the race by leading 130 of the 200 laps. Ward's dominance didn't end in May but continued with victories at Milwaukee, DuQuoin, and the Hoosier Hundred, a late-season race on the one-mile dirt track at the Indiana State Fairgrounds. That was sufficient to gain Ward the US Auto Club's national championship.

"In the next six years they went on a tear like very few people ever went on in IndyCar racing," Miller said. "In six years they won 18 races. They won the Indy 500 in '59 and '62. They won two national championships. . . . Three times they were runner-up for the national championship to A. J. Foyt. . . . Those were the two guys to beat. If you beat Ward you had to beat Foyt and vice versa. When A. J. showed up . . . the yardstick was Rodger Ward. That's who you had to handle."[1]

One significant safety measure was mandated for the 1959 Indy 500 when the USAC required all cars to have roll bars. The roll bar extended above the driver's head and offered protection should the car turn upside down.[2]

A record 16 cars were still running after 500 miles.

Bobby Grim won Rookie of the Year honors by qualifying fifth fastest, but his car had magneto failure after 85 laps and began coasting to the pits. As was customary at that time, Grim raised his arm to signal to other drivers that he had lost power. However, Grim dislocated his arm due to the high air speed.

Grim's crew thought the raised arm was a signal that he needed a relief driver and rushed Jack Turner into the cockpit as Grim exited the car. Naturally, Turner couldn't get the car to start.[3]

Ward won the 1959 race by outdueling runner-up Jim Rathmann and pole-sitter Johnny Thomson. Veteran Tony Bettenhausen came in fourth, and former motorcycle ace Paul Goldsmith was fifth.

Defending champion Jimmy Bryan finished last after engine failure on the first lap.

Rookie Don Branson qualified 10th fastest and finished 24th when his suspension failed. Known as the "racing grandfather," Branson drove in his first 500 at age 38 and finished fourth in 1960 and fifth in 1963.

At age 45, Branson was the oldest driver in the US Auto Club when he and fellow driver Dick Atkins were killed on November 12, 1966, in a fiery accident in a sprint car race at Ascot Park in Gardena, California.

40

Dick Is Jim and Jim Is Dick

JIM RATHMANN MAY HAVE BEEN THE MOST UNDERRATED RACE DRIVER of all time. Not only did he win the 1960 Indy 500, but he also was runner-up in 1952, 1957, and 1959. The only other driver with similar numbers was Bill Holland, with three seconds and a win in 1949.

Rathmann made 14 starts at Indianapolis and finished in the top 10 seven times, but before finishing second to Pat Flaherty in 1956 he failed to place higher than 20th. He started three races in the top 20, including the '60 race when he outdueled Rodger Ward in one of the most competitive races in 500 history.

Rathmann began driving champ cars in 1949, and he led a total of 153 laps at Indianapolis, including 100 in his 1960 victory. That race featured 29 lead changes, with Rathmann and Ward running together most of the second half. Rathmann took the lead for keeps with three laps remaining after Ward was forced to back off because of tire wear. Rathmann's victory margin was 12.75 seconds.

Eddie Sachs won the pole with a four-lap speed of 146.592 mph, but rookie Jim Hurtubise turned in a single lap of 149.601 on the fourth day of qualifying, the biggest challenge yet to the 150-mph lap.

Ward took the lead on the first lap, and Sachs, Rathmann, and former winner Troy Ruttman also led in the early going. The first 47 laps of the race were caution free. The second half saw Johnny Thomson challenge until his car lost power and finished fifth. Ward took his final lead on lap 194, but an earlier stall in the pits had forced him to put excess wear on his tires and to back off.[1]

Jim Rathmann was born Royal Richard Rathmann, the younger brother of fellow Indy driver Dick Rathmann. The two exchanged names in 1946 because the younger brother was too young at 16 to get a racing license. It was meant to be a short-time change, but neither decided to change back.[2]

The 1958 Indy 500 saw Jim finish fifth behind Bryan, Amick, Boyd, and Bettenhausen. Only Boyd and Rathmann survived to the end of their careers. Dick Rathmann started on the pole and came in 27th following the first-lap accident.

The renamed Jim Rathmann settled in Melbourne, Florida, where he operated a Chevrolet dealership and became friends of astronauts Alan Shepard, Gus Grissom, and Gordon Cooper. Rathmann was a frequent visitor to Indianapolis for the race until his death in 2011 at age 83.[3]

41

Ward Walks Away

LIKE BOXERS, RACE DRIVERS SOMETIMES RETIRE AND LATER COME OUT of retirement.

Not Rodger Ward.

Ward's last Indianapolis 500 was in 1966, when he experienced poor handling and pulled into the pits on lap 74 to tell his crew he was retiring on the spot. He kept his word until his death at age 83.

Besides winning the 500 in 1959 and 1962, Ward had a six-year period in which he also finished second twice, third once, and fourth once. The time trials in 1962 had seen Parnelli Jones turn in the first 150-mph lap at the track. The first lap in his four-lap run was scored at 150.720 mph, and his overall speed was 150.370.

Jones, who would win the following year, led the first 59 laps of the race. Over the 200 laps the Leader Card team was as dominant as ever, with Ward and Len Sutton finishing one-two. The teammates were the first to come in first and second since Mauri Rose and Bill Holland in '47 and '48.

Ward was a native of Kansas who moved to Los Angeles as a youth and at 14 built a hot rod with parts from his father's wrecking and junkyard business. He was a pilot in the Army Air Force during World War II and returned to Southern California to race midget cars.[1]

The early years of Ward's career were largely unsuccessful, and his crash following an axle breaking led to Bill Vukovich's fatal crash in 1955.

Ward told the *New York Times* in a 1999 interview that he first met Vukovich at a midget track in Phoenix.

"He came over and said, 'You know, kid, you might become a race driver someday if you stay alive.'"[2]

42

Major Celebrities Missed Race

SOME 25 RACE DRIVERS DID NOT MAKE THE 1958 INDIANAPOLIS 500. They included former winners Troy Ruttman and Pat Flaherty, former world champion Juan Manuel Fangio, former 500 Rookie of the Year Jimmy Daywalt, and Carroll Shelby, later one of the great names in auto racing.

Shelby, who was 35 at the time, didn't even begin his rookie test at the Speedway and never tried to race there again. Shelby became an American icon as an automobile designer and entrepreneur and was best known for his involvement with the AC Cobra and Mustang performance cars. The Mustang became known in America as the Shelby Mustang.[1]

Shelby began racing sports cars and spread his wings to setting 16 US and international speed records at the Bonneville Salt Flats in Utah. He set a record in the Mount Washington Hill Climb and won that event in 1956.[2]

Shelby was named *Sports Illustrated's* Driver of the Year in 1956 and 1957 and competed in eight Formula One races in 1958 and 1959.

Shelby's driving career peaked in 1959 when he co-drove an Aston Martin DBR1 to victory in the 24 Hours of Le Mans.[3]

He retired as a driver in 1959 and opened a high-performance driving school.[4] He made his real mark designing various auto models for the major factories.

Juan Manuel Fangio was a 46-year-old native of Argentina when he opted to make a possible run in the Indianapolis 500 in 1958. Fangio dominated Formula One racing by winning the world championship five times.[5]

His five world championships remained the record for 47 years until Michael Schumacher exceeded it. Fangio proved his mettle with four different teams: Alfa Romeo, Ferrari, Mercedes-Benz, and Maserati. Fangio won 24 of the 52 Formula One races he entered and is the only Argentine driver to win the Argentine Grand Prix, having done that a record four times.[6]

The world champion had witnessed the 500 in 1948 and thereafter expressed interested in racing at Indy. In 1958 he struggled to reach a competitive speed, topping out at 142 mph.

Fangio retired shortly after his brief showing in Indianapolis.

His greatest danger probably didn't occur at any race track but at the Hotel Lincoln in Havana a year after he won the 1957 non-Formula One Grand Prix there. He was favored to win in 1958 when two men kidnapped him at gunpoint. Fangio was held for 29 hours and, on release, remained friends with his captors. He died in 1995 at age 84.

Pat Flaherty, who won the 1956 Indy 500 in a John Zink–owned roadster prepared by master mechanic A. J. Watson, had replaced 1955 winner Bob Sweikert in the car after Sweikert left the team.

Flaherty led 127 of the 200 laps in a race that saw numerous accidents but no serious injuries. Flaherty followed up the Indy race by winning a 100-miler at Milwaukee but was injured that August and was sidelined for two years. He was deemed unable to drive in the 1958 Indianapolis race and died in 2002 at age 76.[7]

The memory of Troy Ruttman in Victory Lane is etched in the memories of everyone who was around racing in 1952.

He was 22 years old, still the youngest to win at Indianapolis. He wore an old-fashioned helmet of the day, and his 250 pounds appeared to be struggling to get out of his six foot three body. He stood in the cockpit of his cream and red Agajanian Special with flames painted on the race car. In those days the Speedway brought in a Hollywood movie star to kiss the winner, and Ruttman looked as if he might never let go of stunning redhead Arlene Dahl.

On that day Ruttman was the benefactor of racing luck. In subsequent years, when many believed he would make multiple trips to the winner's circle, Troy didn't have much luck at all.

Ruttman broke in as a 500 rookie in 1949 and won three years later when Bill Vukovich's pace-setting car broke down with nine laps to go. Ruttman, who was charging but well behind, became an unexpected winner.

Years later Ruttman admitted that the win was a "classic case of too much too soon."[8]

Ruttman was a born racer, admittedly getting his first traffic ticket at age nine.[9]

He was so good racing around Southern California that he made the Indy field at 19. When he retired from racing he was only 34, probably considered an underachiever by many.

"In 1949 he's 19 years old. He goes to Salem three times and wins all three races. He goes to Dayton and races four times and wins three of them. He goes to Winchester once and wins it," recalled Robin Miller of *Racer* magazine. "He races eight times on the high banks and is 19 years old and he wins seven of them."

Ruttman ran 21 races in 1951 and won 16 of them while finishing second four times and third once.[10]

Having seen his share of troubles racing, Ruttman suffered his biggest heartache when his son, Troy Jr., died in a racing accident. Cancer brought along his own death in 1997.

Jimmy Daywalt was the 500's Rookie of the Year in 1953 when he finished sixth. Daywalt made 20 starts on the circuit between 1950 and 1962 and had a trio of top-three finishes. A native of Wabash, Indiana, he was one of the most popular Indy drivers, enjoying a special rapport with his home-state fans.

Jimmy ran in eight 500s but didn't compete in the 1958 event. His second-best finish was ninth in 1955, and he was the second fastest qualifier in 1954. Jimmy died of cancer at age 41.

Eddie Russo, the nephew of race driver Paul Russo, qualified for the race in 1955, 1957, and 1960 and was a relief driver in 1956. Russo's father, Joe, lost his life at Langhorne only days after finishing fifth in the 1934 Indianapolis 500.

Eddie was in line to qualify a second Novi in 1956 when rain washed away his chance of making the race. A second Novi driven by Uncle Paul led until crashing in the first turn.

Eddie Russo made 21 starts in champ cars before losing an eye in the 1960 Indy 500, which ended his driving career. He died in 2012 at age 86.[11]

Freddie Agabashian drove 1,273 laps in the Indianapolis 500 and led one of them, which didn't keep him from becoming one of the Speedway's most popular figures.

Agabashian's name forever is linked to the Cummins Diesel Special, an extraordinary vehicle that sat on the pole in 1952. Already having driven in 11 Indy races, Agabashian was at the track in 1958, but it turned out that his final race was in 1957.

Five years earlier Agabashian and his unique car had set the racing world on its ear with a qualifying speed of 138.010 mph. Fans were not so impressed by its speed but by the fact that the low-slung, diesel-powered car was the most unusual sounding and looking car in the field. Brown in color, the Cummins Diesel looked for all the world like a cigar

At the time Agabashian was a personable veteran of five Indianapolis races who had finished ninth as a rookie but hadn't finished a race since. The Cummins Diesel lasted only 71 laps because of a clogged air intake and finished 27th.[12]

After that disappointment Agabashian finished fourth and sixth the next two years, but the diesel never returned. In 1959 Freddie became an analyst on the Indianapolis Motor Speedway Radio Network.

43

Dick, the Other Rathmann

VERY FEW BROTHER ACTS IN SPORTS RESULT IN THE SIBLINGS HAVING comparable careers. So it was with Dick and Jim Rathmann, who both had lengthy careers as race drivers.

Jim Rathmann won the 1960 Indianapolis 500 and had three runner-up finishes in the race. Dick, the older of the two, drove more than one thousand laps in the 500 but mostly is remembered for one—the first one of the 1958 race.

Sitting on the pole, Dick took the lead in the first turn and held it until the end of the backstretch when Ed Elisian passed him entering the third turn.

Rathmann and Elisian had been the two fastest qualifiers and, at least under the surface, there was an intense desire to lead the first lap. Valerie Bettenhausen, the widow of Tony, said years later in an ESPN interview that everyone feared an accident:

"Everybody knew it was going to happen; there was so much needling," she said. "Those two guys in the first row, Dick and Ed. Everybody talked about it. What a first turn, what a first lap this is gonna be. And it happened. I remember it like it was yesterday because they each were going to lead that first lap, and look what happened."[1]

Maybe if Rathmann had lifted his foot off the accelerator a couple of seconds sooner, Elisian also would have slowed sooner for the turn, but almost everyone blamed Elisian for driving too far into the corner. He lost control, his car slammed into Rathmann's, and the track was blocked to almost everyone behind them.

Rathmann consistently qualified well for the 500, but his pole speed of 145.974 mph in 1958 was his biggest moment. Rathmann's inability to finish the first lap made him one of three pole-sitters to go out before the first lap ended. Roberto Guerrero spun out on the pace lap in 1992, and Scott Sharp hit the wall in the first turn in 2001.

In 1956, his second year at the Speedway, Rathmann started on the inside of the second row. For the next three years after the crash he qualified fourth quickest twice and sixth quickest once. He finished the race fifth in '56 and seventh in '64, but mechanical problems took him out of six other races.[2]

Rathmann missed the 1957 race for a most unusual reason. He had qualified but was mugged the night before the race, and Johnnie Parsons took his place in the car.[3]

Rathman moved to NASCAR in 1951 but returned to champ cars in 1955.

44

Hollywood Comes to Indy

THE GLAMOUR AND SUSPENSE OF AUTOMOBILE RACING WAS BOUND TO appeal to Hollywood sooner or later—and the attraction usually was built around danger.

The movies first featured the Speedway in 1929, which coincided with the Great Depression. A movie named *Speedway* came out that year as one of the last silent films, which means a major attraction of auto racing (roaring engines) could not be part of the appeal. William Haines starred in the comedy, along with Anita Page. The movie was shot in Indianapolis.[1]

The *Big Wheel* was produced in 1949 and featured live footage of the 1949 race. The actual racing footage was realistic, but the rest bore little resemblance to the actual event.

Mickey Rooney was the star as Billy Coy, a race driver whose father had been killed. Thomas Mitchell played his crew chief, and Spring Byington was Billy's mother. The ending may be the worst in movie history, as 500 winner Bill Holland was so impressed by Billy Coy's courage that he gives him the winner's Borg-Warner Trophy.

The *Big Wheel* was the first movie to incorporate into a film the fiery 1949 crash of Duke Nalon. None of these movies would have surfaced without the danger element.

Donald Davidson interviewed Rooney years later and quoted him in the 2004 race program. "I did some real stinkers and *The Big Wheel* was one of them," Rooney said.[2]

To Please a Lady was also shot in Indianapolis in 1950 and introduced Clark Gable to the Hoosier capital. Gable already had been to the track: a famous photo of the 1947 flying start showed him sitting in the first row in the first turn, arguably the best seat in the house. In 1950 his co-star, Barbara Stanwyck, was brought to the race by the Speedway management to kiss the winning driver in Victory Lane. Johnnie Parsons was the lucky winner.

Hollywood launched some major racing movies, beginning in 1966 with *Grand Prix*. The plot emphasized the danger of the sport and centered on the death of the Yves Montand character and the grieving reaction of Eva Marie Saint, his squeeze in the movie.

Many racing fans were able to ignore the romantic angle in the picture and concentrate on the excellent camera work that put them inside a race car.

Probably the purest racing movie ever made was *Le Mans,* starring Steve McQueen. Much of it was filmed during the annual 24-hour endurance race in Le Mans, France. The plot is woven through the racing action and involves an American driver haunted by the memory of a prior accident. The movie has a minimum of conversation and, instead, lets the intense racing action carry the plot.

Winning probably is the best movie about the Indy 500. It stars Paul Newman, Joanne Woodward, and Robert Wagner in a love triangle. It is set almost totally around the Speedway area, including the Speedway Motel that once bordered the track.

The pre-race action is magnificently covered, including the band music, last-minute engine adjustment, and the atmosphere as race time approaches. A subtle, but strong moment shows Newman climbing into his race car and taking a deep breath to relieve the tension before the race.

The producers used the multi-car accident at the start of the 1966 race to increase the drama of the film.

His appearance in *Winning* led Newman to launch a career in racing himself, one in which he was a successful race driver and also co-owner of one of the top teams in Indy car racing. Newman was a frequent competitor in Sports Car Club of America races. He teamed with Carl Haas to form Newman-Haas Racing, whose drivers included Mario and Michael Andretti and Nigel Mansell.

45

Fans Fall to Their Death

THOUSANDS OF RACING FANS WHO FLOCKED INTO THE INFIELD OF THE 2.5-mile Speedway had little or no view of the race cars. Some of the wildest party animals didn't care, but some of those who wanted a cheaper look at the race built their own viewing positions. Scaffolding materials more often used for construction work were hauled to the Speedway and assembled so occupants could see a decent portion of the track.

This practice came to a tragic conclusion in 1960 when one of the scaffolds collapsed during the pace lap. Killed were Fred Linder, 36, of Indianapolis, and William Craig, 37, of Zionsville. About 125 spectators were on the scaffold when it collapsed as the fans changed position to watch the cars. The tower was about 30 feet high and was erected by an individual not connected with the Speedway. The following year the Speedway management disallowed the structures.[1]

The spectators had paid five or ten dollars to watch the race from the structure. More than 80 fans were injured, including some on the ground, and about 22 suffered serious injuries.

Among witnesses to the accident was future three-time winner Johnny Rutherford, who was at the race as a fan. His future wife, Betty Hoyer, was a student nurse who helped the injured.

46

Goldsmith Was Multi-dimensional

PAUL GOLDSMITH WAS A MASTER OF THE TWO-WHEELER BEFORE mastering the four-wheel vehicle. Give him a unicycle and he probably would have beaten the competition.

How good was Paul Goldsmith? Robin Miller recalled a conversation with A. J. Foyt in which Foyt said, "Paul Goldsmith is the most underappreciated bad ass I ever raced against."[1]

Goldsmith, who at the time of this writing lives in northern Indiana at age 92, was one of the lucky ones at Indianapolis on May 30, 1958. Jerry Unser's car left a tire mark on Goldsmith's back as it sailed over the third-turn wall. Goldsmith drove one of the eight cars knocked out of the race.

Several years before his debut at Indianapolis, Goldsmith was a star with the American Motorcycle Association. Often competing against Joe Leonard, who would win the pole at Indianapolis in 1968, Goldsmith manhandled his Harley-Davidson to five AMA National victories between 1952 and 1955. He captured the Daytona 200 in 1953, then retired from the two-wheelers to concentrate on auto racing. Goldsmith won the final NASCAR race on the beach at Daytona in 1958, the same year he was a rookie at Indianapolis.

A native of Parkersburg, West Virginia, Goldsmith moved to Detroit with his family as a teenager. He didn't ride a motorcycle until after World War II and quickly graduated into racing cycles on flat-dirt tracks. While Goldsmith displayed a hot foot driving Indy cars, it was even hotter sticking his left foot into the dirt while he navigated corners on a cycle.

"The first race I ever entered was in Marshall, Michigan. They didn't have enough experts so they let me (an amateur) ride in that race and I finished third," Goldsmith said later. "They never let me go back down and race in the amateurs after that."[2]

Beginning in 1947, Goldsmith won a number of races at various county fairs and soon began excelling at higher levels, despite still working at the Chrysler plant in Detroit. At one point he was asked to help a youngster named Joe Leonard learn the ropes, and Leonard became his toughest opponent.

"There was very little glamour in racing those days. We all slept in our cars, but we had a great time," Goldsmith was quoted by the AMA.[3]

Goldsmith had moved mostly to stock cars by 1955 and turned to NASCAR, where he was an immediate flash when he wasn't also winning in US Auto Club stock cars. Over 11 years he won nine NASCAR races and had 22 top-10 finishes. He ran eight champ car races between 1958 and 1965.

Goldsmith returned to Indianapolis a year after the third-turn accident and finished fifth. The next year he was third behind the dueling Jim Rathmann and Rodger Ward. In his three final 500s he had parts fail during the race.

After retiring in 1969, Goldsmith ran an aviation business in northern Indiana.

47

The Lady Lost Her Life

AUTO RACING CHANGED FOREVER IN 1976 WHEN CAR OWNER ROLLA
Vollstedt invited Janet Guthrie to test-drive a car at the Indianapolis Motor
Speedway. Guthrie's credentials included being a licensed pilot, flight instruc-
tor, and aerospace engineer. She had never driven at Langhorne or Milwaukee,
and the male intelligentsia was quick to dismiss her chances to drive in the
500.[1]

Later that year Guthrie became the first woman to drive in a NASCAR
Winston Cup super speedway stock car race. A year later she drove in both the
Indianapolis 500 and the Daytona 500.

Not only did the Indianapolis Motor Speedway include her in its list of history's top 100 drivers, but her helmet and suit are on display in the Smithsonian
Institution. Guthrie ran in three Indy 500s and finished eighth in 1978.

Guthrie was followed at Indianapolis by Lyn St. James in 1992, who competed in eight races. Then came Sarah Fisher in 2000 and Danica Patrick in
2005. Patrick became a national celebrity when as a rookie she led the 500 in its
waning laps. She later won an IndyCar Series race in Japan and, after switching
to NASCAR, sat on the pole for the Daytona 500.

That started a trend of women drivers in open-wheel racing. Katherine
Legge raced against the best open-wheel drivers and walked away from a serious accident in 2006. Milka Duno raced three times at Indianapolis but never
ran close to the front. Pippa Mann has been an IndyCar Series regular, and

Ana Beatriz raced at Indy four times. Simona de Silvestro has run at Indy since 2010.

As more women entered the sport it was inevitable that some of them would get hurt. Pippa Mann was involved in the horrific accident that killed Dan Wheldon. De Silvestro drove in the 500 with serious burns. Kara Hendricks might well have been racing on the same track were it not for an accident in El Cajon, California, in 1991.

Hendricks was driving in a US Auto Club midget race at the Cajon Speedway. She died later at a San Diego-area hospital of head injuries. She had driven in more than 100 races.

Hendricks finished second in the three-quarter midget point standings in 1989, the highest any woman has attained. On the night she was killed she set a course record of 15.75 seconds for three-eighths of a mile. Hendricks's throttle stuck on the second lap of the feature race, and her car flipped several times.[2]

48

Indy among Top-10 Dangerous Tracks

THE WEBSITE *THERICHEST.COM* SELECTED WHAT IT TERMED THE 10 deadliest racetracks in the world. Eight of the 10 aren't in the United States; the exceptions are Indianapolis at number three and Daytona at number six.

While Indianapolis is older than any of the other tracks, its fatality rate (56 since 1909) stands out. The website explains its rating as follows:

> The 2.5-mile track is a rectangular oval with two long straights. The longer 5/8 mile stretches allow for cars to increase speed greatly. Average speeds can be anywhere in the range of 160–230 miles per hour depending on the competition. In the track's early years the speed was usually much lower but still high enough to cause problems.
>
> A number of cars rolled during this period, often killing the driver and riding mechanic. As speeds increased, crashes came about from loss of traction, usually in the corners. Cars either struck the wall or struck other cars, killing and injuring drivers. That said, the last race car related fatality for a driver came in 2003 when Tony Renna lost control of his vehicle and caught the fence.[1]

The two racetracks rated as more dangerous than Indy were Isle of Man/ Snefell Mountain and Nürburgring, both European tracks.

49

The Former Winner's Last Race

THE 33-CAR STARTING LINEUP FOR THE 1958 INDIANAPOLIS 500 FEATURED only one former winner, 1950 champion Johnnie Parsons. Parsons, who also had been runner-up to Bill Holland in 1949, started the race from the outside of the second row and finished 12th. It would be the final 500 for the 10-year veteran.

Parsons, a Californian, started his career driving midgets, and once he reached the Indy circuit blew away the competition. From 1946 through 1952 he won 11 national championship events, scoring one win in 1948, five while en route to the 1949 driving championship, two in both 1950 and 1951, and a single win in 1952. Parsons won the season finale three straight years, including one at the new Darlington Raceway in South Carolina.[1]

As a youngster, Parsons sold programs at the Gilmore Stadium midget track and was hired by Frank Kurtis, whose car Parsons would drive to victory at Indianapolis. That race was shortened by rain to 345 miles, possibly a break for Parsons. His crew reportedly found a crack in the engine block the morning of the race and there was doubt the car would have lasted 500 miles.

Parsons died in 1984 at age 66 at his home in Van Nuys, California. His son, Johnny Parsons, drove in 12 Indy races between 1974 and 1996. Johnny's parents divorced, and his mother married race driver Duane Carter. Johnny was a half brother of another Indy racer, Pancho Carter.

The engraver etching Johnnie's name on the Borg-Warner Trophy made a mistake, spelling it "Johnny."

50

Death Wasn't Only
Bad Result

RACE DRIVER BOB HURT DIED ON SEPTEMBER 27, 2000. THERE MUST have been times when he wished death had occurred 32 years sooner.

Hurt was an ambitious youngster with a bright future when he crashed at the Indianapolis Motor Speedway on May 27, 1968. It occurred after an extra day was allotted for qualifying because weather had prevented potential qualifiers from filling the field.

Hurt was injured during morning practice and was taken to nearby Methodist Hospital. He spent two months there before being transferred to the Rusk Institute of Rehabilitation Medicine in New York. He had lost movement in much of his body.

For the next 32 years Hurt tirelessly studied about living with paralysis, and he talked with those with similar problems, including actor Christopher Reeve and race driver Sam Schmidt. His life ended after 61 years while he was sleeping alone in a Toronto hotel.[1]

While Hurt continued to visit the Speedway, Schmidt stayed in racing as a successful car owner. Sam didn't drive professionally until he was 31, but he made the field for the 500 in 1997 at age 32. In 1999, after three Indy appearances, he won a race in Las Vegas. During the winter he was testing at Walt Disney World Speedway when a crash left him a quadriplegic. He spent five months on a ventilator.[2]

Schmidt later formed Schmidt Motorsports, which became the most successful team in the Indy Lights series, a stepping-stone for drivers to the IndyCar Series. In 2011 Alex Tagliani won the pole for the Indy 500 in a Schmidt car.[3]

51

Most Great Indy
Drivers Survived

THE INDIANAPOLIS MOTOR SPEEDWAY CONDUCTED A CAMPAIGN IN 2011 to determine the top drivers in Speedway history. The Speedway called an "esteemed panel of international motorsports media veterans" to evaluate all 732 race veterans and select the top 100.

The Speedway then asked race fans to narrow the 100 to the 33 best drivers of all time. The top eight drivers selected by the fans are still living or died natural deaths. Bill Vukovich was judged to be the best driver to die in a racing accident. Others in the top 33 who died racing were Jim Clark, number 18; Mark Donohue, number 22; and Tony Bettenhausen, number 32.

The results, and brief biographical information follows:

1. A. J. FOYT

Foyt competed in a record 35 consecutive Indianapolis 500s and was the first to win four times: 1961, 1964, 1967, and 1977. Foyt also won the pole four times and led a record 13 races for a total of 555 laps. He is the only one to win the 500 in both front- and rear-engine cars. A rookie in 1958, Foyt retired on pole day in 1993. He also won the race as a car owner with Kenny Brack in 1999.

2. RICK MEARS

Mears first won in 1979 and added victories in 1984, 1988, and 1991. The Californian won his four victories in only 14 attempts, while Foyt needed 20 and Al Unser required 22. Mears won the pole six times and sat on the front row 11 times. Serious foot injuries in an accident made it hard for Mears to drive on road courses, but his record at Indianapolis is almost unequaled.

3. AL UNSER

Unser made 27 starts at the Speedway and won in 1970, 1971, 1978, and 1987. Unser led 644 laps in 11 races and ranks second in miles completed. He dominated the 1970 race by leading 190 of the 200 laps from the pole position. Unser was known for taking care of his car, as evidenced by the 18 times his car was running at the finish of the race.

4. BOBBY UNSER

Bobby was the first Unser brother to win the race when he outdueled the turbine-powered cars of Joe Leonard and Graham Hill in 1968. He also won in 1975 and 1981. Unser won the pole in 1972, posting a speed 17 mph faster than the 1971 pole speed.

5. HELIO CASTRONEVES

Helio is one of the most popular Indy drivers ever, a reputation personified by his climbing the fence after victories and by winning the competition on the *Dancing with the Stars* television show. Castroneves has sat on the pole four times and won the race in 2001, 2002, and 2009.

6. JOHNNY RUTHERFORD

Nicknamed Lone Star J. R., the Texas native was a rookie in 1963 and didn't finish higher than 18th until 1973. He then won the race in 1974, 1976, and 1980, leading the most laps on each occasion.

7. MARIO ANDRETTI

Andretti was Rookie of the Year in 1965 when he finished third. Mario became an annual contender to win the race but, except for winning in 1969, had terrible luck at Indianapolis. Andretti won the pole three times and finished second twice. He led a total of 556 laps in 29 races and was constantly besieged by problems. "Mario is slowing down" became a catchphrase.

8. WILBUR SHAW

Shaw won the 500 in 1937, 1939, and 1940, but his major contribution to the Indianapolis 500 was facilitating the sale of the Speedway to Tony Hulman at the end of World War II. He then served as the track's president until his death in a plane crash in 1954.

9. BILL VUKOVICH
(Killed racing)

Vukovich won the 1953 and 1954 races and was leading in 1955 when he came on a multi-car crash on the backstretch and died when his car flipped multiple times outside the track. He also was leading in 1952 when his car failed in the final 10 laps. Vukovich led 485 of the 647 laps from 1952 to 1955.

10. EMERSON FITTIPALDI
Fittipaldi had won two world championships in Formula One before he came to Indianapolis. Fittipaldi became an instant fan favorite and won the 500 in 1989 and 1993. His late-race duel with Al Unser Jr. in 1989 is a 500 classic; after the two touched wheels in the third turn, Unser slammed hard into the wall. Fittipaldi bypassed the Indianapolis tradition of drinking milk in Victory Lane by switching to orange juice. Emmo, as he came to be known in America, led seven races for a total of 505 laps. Fittipaldi's racing career ended in 1996 following a serious accident at the Michigan International Speedway.

11. AL UNSER JR.
Al Junior, occasionally called Little Al, won the 1992 race by .043 of a second over Scott Goodyear and repeated the win in 1994. Al Junior raced in 19 Indy races, with seven finishes in the top 10. He's the son of four-time winner Al and nephew of three-time winner Bobby.

12. LOUIE MEYER
Meyer was the first three-time winner of the 500, coming in first in 1928, 1933, and 1936. In his 12 races he also finished second once and third twice.

13. MAURI ROSE
Rose won the 1941 race as a relief driver for Floyd Davis. His star rose after the war when he won back-to-back races in one of Lou Moore's Blue Crown Spark Plug Specials. Mauri had six top-three finishes in 15 races.

14. PARNELLI JONES
Jones made only seven starts in the 500, winning in 1963 and leading in five of his seven appearances. He was the first to record a 150-mph lap in qualifying. He dominated the 1967 race in a turbine-powered machine that failed four laps from the finish.

15. GORDON JOHNCOCK
Johncock is best remembered for beating out a charging Rick Mears by 0.16 of a second in 1982. He previously won the rain-shortened and crash-dominated 1973 race. Johncock made 24 starts in the race and finished 10 times in the top six.

16. ARIE LUYENDYK
The Dutchman recorded victories at Indianapolis in 1990 and 1997. His average speed of 185.081 mph in 1990 remains the race record. Luyendyk won the pole three times and started in the front row five times.

17. RODGER WARD
Ward had a string of six races in which he finished fourth or better, including victories in 1959 and 1962. He finished second to Jim Rathmann in 1960 when tire wear forced him to back off in the final laps. Ward ran in the race only 15 times and retired as a driver in the middle of the 1966 race.

18. JIM CLARK
(Killed racing)
The Flying Scot was a two-time world champion who finished second in his debut at the Speedway in 1963. Clark drove five races at Indianapolis and led the race in four of them. He was the winner in 1965, when he led 190 of the 200 laps. Clark was killed on April 7, 1968, during a race in Hockenheim, Germany.

19. DARIO FRANCHITTI
Besides winning the 500 in 2007, 2010, and 2012, the Scotland native was the IndyCar Series champion four times. Franchitti posted 21 victories in his Indy-Car Series career and won 10 more while driving champ cars. He retired after suffering serious injuries in a 2013 race in Houston, Texas.

20. TOM SNEVA
Sneva was the first driver to turn a 200-mph lap at the Speedway, in 1977. That marked the first of three times Sneva sat on the pole. He won the 1983 race from the pole after leading 98 laps. Sneva was runner-up in the race three times, including 1980 when he started in the 33rd, or last, position.

21. BOBBY RAHAL

Rahal won the 1986 race by passing Kevin Cogan on a restart with two laps to go and is the only driver to turn the quickest lap of the race on the final lap. Bobby won three CART series championships and finished in the top seven at the 500 seven times. His car owner, Jim Trueman, died eleven days after Rahal's Indy victory.

22. MARK DONOHUE

(Killed racing)

Donohue was the first driver fielded by car owner Roger Penske in the 1960s, and in 1972 he recorded the first of Penske's 16 Indy victories. Donohue, a graduate of Brown University, started three times from the front row and finished second in 1970. Donohue died in Graz, Austria, on August 19, 1975, following a practice session crash in which he first appeared not to be badly hurt. He went to the hospital the next day, lapsed into a coma, and died.

23. MICHAEL ANDRETTI

Michael Andretti probably was one of the best drivers never to win the Indianapolis 500. He competed 16 times, with a second-place finish in 1991. Michael, the son of Mario, led a total of 431 laps at Indy, including 97 in 1991. Andretti became a highly successful car owner after retiring.

24. RALPH DEPALMA

DePalma led 196 laps in the 1912 race but didn't win because of engine failure on the final lap. He unsuccessfully tried to push his car across the finish line. DePalma led 612 laps at the Speedway, which still is second to Al Unser. He won the 500 in 1915.

25. RAY HARROUN

Harroun was only 32 years old when he won the inaugural 500 in 1911, yet that was the last time he competed at the track. He is credited with being the first to use a rear-view mirror.

26. TOMMY MILTON

Milton won the race in 1923 following an earlier triumph in 1921, which made him the 500's first double winner. He competed in eight races and led a total of 218 laps.

27. DANNY SULLIVAN

The handsome Kentuckian is mostly known for his "spin and win" in 1985. While passing Mario Andretti coming out of the first turn Sullivan spun in the south chute but maintained control without hitting the wall and continued on to victory. Sullivan recorded four other top-10 finishes in his 12 races.

28. GRAHAM HILL

The Brit won two Formula One world championships and ran only three times at Indianapolis, winning as a rookie in 1966. Driving a turbine-powered car in 1968, he became the first to record a 170-mph qualifying lap. He was killed in a plane crash on November 29, 1975, in Elstree, England.

29. DAN GURNEY

Gurney had a successful driving career that didn't include winning at Indianapolis, but his firm designed and built the All American Racers team that won in 1968 and 1975. Gurney also was behind the merger of Lotus and Ford that preceded Jim Clark's win in 1965.

30. JIM RATHMANN

Rathmann won the 1960 Indy 500 and was second in 1952, 1957, and 1959. He also started three races from the front row.

31. JUAN PABLO MONTOYA

Montoya is a veteran of Formula One, Indy car, and NASCAR who won the 500 in 2000 as a rookie and won again in 2015. In his first win he started from the pole and led 167 laps.

32. TONY BETTENHAUSEN

(Killed racing)

Tony made 14 starts and was one of the favorites in 1961 when he was killed in a spectacular crash during a practice session at the Speedway. Bettenhausen was runner-up to Bob Sweikert in the 1955 race and finished in the top four three times.

33. SCOTT DIXON

The native of New Zealand won the IndyCar Series championship twice and captured the Indy 500 in 2008. He remains one of the top drivers in the series.

Others named in the media list of 100 were, listed alphabetically:

Freddie Agabashian, Marco Andretti, Billy Arnold, Cliff Bergere, Gary Bettenhausen, Johnny Boyd, Joe Boyer, Jimmy Bryan, Eddie Cheever Jr., Art Cross, Bill Cummings, Gil de Ferran, Peter DePaolo, Pat Flaherty, Fred Frame, Scott Goodyear, Robby Gordon, Jules Goux, Roberto Guerrero, Janet Guthrie, Sam Hanks, Harry Hartz, Ralph Hepburn, Bill Holland, Ted Horn, Sam Hornish Jr., Jim Hurtubise, Tony Kanaan, Ray Keech, Mel Kenyon, Buddy Lazier, Joe Leonard, Frank Lockhart, Nigel Mansell, Bobby Marshman, Rex Mays, Roger McCluskey, Jim McElreath, Jack McGrath, Chet Miller, Mike Mosley, Ralph Mulford, Jimmy Murphy, Duke Nalon, Pat O'Connor, Barney Oldfield, Danny Ongais, Johnnie Parsons, Danica Patrick, Dario Resta, Peter Revson, Lloyd Ruby, Troy Ruttman, Eddie Sachs, Jimmy Snyder, George Souders, Jackie Stewart, Tony Stewart, Bob Sweikert, Rene Thomas, Johnny Thomson, Paul Tracy, Jacques Villeneuve, Bill Vukovich II, Lee Wallard, Dan Wheldon, Howdy Wilcox.

52

Mario Survives Spectacular Flip

MARIO ANDRETTI IS THE TYPE OF RACE DRIVER ONE FEARED WOULD suffer a tragic ending. He raced successfully in all types of cars, from Formula One to Indy cars to stock cars to sports cars. He always was among the most aggressive drivers, yet he avoided accidents that might have ended his career.

As Andretti frequently said, "If everything seems under control you're just not going fast enough."

Andretti won the 1969 Indy 500, the 1967 Daytona 500, and the 1978 Formula One world championship. Like Barney Oldfield at the turn of the century, Mario's name was synonymous with racing. Many a police officer has stopped a speeder with the words, "Who do you think you are, Mario Andretti?"

Mario retired from auto racing after the 1994 season amid much fanfare. But nine years after his retirement he was involved in one of the most spectacular accidents in Indianapolis history.

Andretti agreed to test-drive a car owned by his son, Michael, and in so doing probably had his closest brush with death. Two minutes before the practice session was to end, Mario went through the first turn trailing Kenny Brack, who crashed and left debris across the track.

Andretti ran on some of the debris entering the south chute and the front end of his car lifted up. The race car began flipping end over end, not unlike a football headed for the goalposts. After at least a half dozen flips the car came down on its wheels and Andretti escaped with only a scratched chin.

"You just have to hope the Man upstairs doesn't forget you." Andretti said.[1]

53

The Most Deadly Sport?

IN THE PUBLIC EYE AUTO RACING IS THE MOST DANGEROUS SPORT, BUT is that really the case?

A story by National Public Radio in 2012 reported that 24 horses a week die at the nation's racetracks. A *New York Times* report said in 2009 that more than 6,600 horses have broken down or showed signs of injury.[1]

OK, as animal lovers we have to sympathize, but what about the perils faced by the jockeys?

Ron Turcotte, jockey for the super horse Secretariat, was paralyzed in 1978 in a racing accident. Billy Haughton, a standout harness racing driver, died in 1986 from injuries sustained in a racing accident at Yonkers, New York. There is a long list of similar incidents.

A medical journal in Australia claimed that a jockey's job is more dangerous than that of a boxer. The study noted that in 75,000 races run one year in Australia there were five jockey deaths and 861 serious injuries.

Granted, American auto races don't total 75,000 in a year.

"Jockeys had a higher risk of fatality than pilots and flight engineers, logging workers, structural metal workers, farm workers, roofers, and truck drivers," Dr. Leigh Blizzard told the *Sydney Morning Herald*.[2]

Another sport that must rival auto racing for danger is unlimited hydroplane racing. Such boating stars as Donald Campbell, Chuck Thompson, Bill Muncey, and Dean Chenoweth are among the big-name drivers who died in hydroplane accidents.

The gridiron also can be a deadly place. In recent years concerns about concussions have risen. An average of 12 high school and college players die annually during practice and games, according to the National Center for Catastrophic Sports Injury Research. The organization recorded 243 football deaths over a 10-year period ending in 2010.

Hockey. Soccer. Track and field. Gymnastics. Cheerleading. They all have occasional injuries of various dimensions. But auto racing is the sport with the deepest reputation of danger, and the sport that requires constant improvements in safety to match its ever increasing perils. The winning speed at the Indianapolis 500 has increased 300 percent since the inaugural race. Auto racing faces not only the biggest dangers but the biggest challenges.

54

The Trials of Cal Niday

FOR MANY YEARS CAL NIDAY LOOKED LIKE A SURVIVOR OF THE RACING game. Niday was almost killed in the waning moments of the 1955 Indy 500 when his car slammed into a fence at the northwest end of the Speedway.

Many fans left the track that day unaware of his accident; their thoughts were locked on Bill Vukovich's fatal crash earlier in the race. Cal suffered a fractured skull that affected his vision, a crushed chest, a ruptured liver, multiple cuts, and third-degree burns that required skin grafts.

Otherwise he was in fairly good shape.

Niday didn't match the race car driver stereotype. He was short, had a mustache, and a wooden leg. He once was a barber.

Niday had once been an athlete, and was expected to play football at Washington State. He took to motorcycles and was president of the Southern California Motorcycle Club when it claimed actors Clark Gable and Ward Bond as members. He worked in a Hollywood movie studio and while working as a stunt biker broke the only good leg he had.

Instead of Washington State he graduated from Moler Barber and Beauty College. Cal Niday was no beauty school dropout.

After his crash in 1955 Niday tried to return to Indianapolis, but his vision was impaired. He still insisted that if he hadn't crashed he might have won the 1955 race.

With three Indianapolis races under his belt, Niday faded away into retirement. Maybe he would never have been heard from again except for a vintage car race on Valentine's Day 1988. While driving in the event at Willow Springs Raceway in California he was thrown from his car when it turned over. He quickly developed an irregular heartbeat and suffered a heart attack en route to the hospital, where he died at age 73.[1]

55

Weyant, the Oldest Survivor

SURVIVORS OF THE 1958 INDIANAPOLIS 500 ARE DOWN TO THREE: A. J. Foyt, Paul Goldsmith, and Chuck Weyant, born in 1923 and the oldest living veteran of an Indy race.[1]

Weyant started in the next-to-last row of the 1958 race after qualifying at 142.608 mph and finished 24th after crashing in the fourth turn on the 38th lap. That was his third 500, following a 12th-place finish in 1955 and a 14th place in 1957.

Weyant ran at Indy again in 1959, finishing 28th after a third-turn crash on lap 45. He hit the outside wall and subsequently was struck by the car of Mike Magill, which turned upside down and slid down the track. Magill suffered serious back injuries.

Weyant, a resident of Springfield, Illinois, recalled carrying around a picture of his race car when he was a soldier during World War II.

"I bet I had that out a thousand times showing it to different guys," Weyant recalled. "I wore the picture out. I was proud of that old race car."[2]

As with many open-wheel drivers of that day, Weyant launched his career racing midgets. He was from a racing family and competed against his brother and father before World War II. He won at least 64 feature races, including 13 national events.[3]

Weyant says making the 500 was his greatest accomplishment.

"You've got a million race car drivers in the United States, and every one reverts back to, 'If I could just make the Speedway,'" Weyant said. "You are one of 33 sitting there in something a million other guys wished that they were doing."[4]

Weyant competed in champ cars from 1952 to 1959, making 21 career starts.

56

Stewart Pushes for Safety

TIME AND IMAGINATION HAVE PAINTED US A PICTURE OF THE STEREO-typical Grand Prix racing driver. First, he is a dashingly handsome European with an alluring accent, a confident air, and impenetrable courage.

He can have any woman he wants—an exception came when James Hunt lost his wife, Suzy, to actor Richard Burton. Still, Hunt apparently was a good negotiator because Burton paid him $1 million to cover Hunt's divorce costs.[1]

The Grand Prix driver has a name like a hero in one of Shakespeare's poems: Alberto Ascari, Juan Manuel Fangio, Lorenzo Bandini. Even America's last Formula One champion had a rhythmic name—Mario Andretti.

Jackie Stewart was, and still is, a stereotypical Grand Prix driver. But he realized that another Grand Prix stereotype, invincibility, was a mirage. Stewart, a former Formula One champion from Scotland, set out to make racing safer. Unlike some of his peers, who probably felt the same, Jackie used his considerable influence to encourage better safety measures.

One calculation suggested that during the time frame he raced, Stewart had a two-thirds chance of being killed in a crash.[2]

Stewart, who drove twice in the Indianapolis 500, directed his attention to the world circuit, but his popularity with Americans could not go unnoticed by US racing organizers. Stewart had one incident that especially motivated him toward improving safety.

In 1966 Stewart was trapped inside his car at Spa in Belgium when Graham Hill abandoned his vehicle to come to his rescue. Jackie was going 165 mph in a heavy rain when he crashed into a telephone pole and shed. His steering column pinned his leg as fuel from his wrecked car poured out. No track officials were nearby and no extradition tools were present. No doctors or medics were around. It was some five minutes before Hill and another man pulled him to safety. Then he lay on a stretcher on a cluttered floor for some time before an ambulance picked him up.[3]

Even then care was delayed because the ambulance driver got lost. Stewart didn't receive proper care until a private jet flew him back to the United Kingdom.

That occurrence led Stewart to launch a campaign to avert avoidable accidents. Stewart felt he was losing too many peers to racing, drivers who included Jim Clark, Jochen Rindt, and François Cevert. On the day Clark was killed in Hockenheim, Germany, Stewart chose to skip that race and conduct a safety inspection at another track.[4]

Stewart retired in 1973, reportedly motivated by an unsatisfactory safety barrier. Stewart was especially shaken by the horrifying 2011 crash in Las Vegas that killed two-time Indy 500 winner Dan Wheldon. Because the spectacular, multi-car accident was witnessed by a large television audience, Stewart hoped it might shake some Formula One drivers out of their alleged complacency.[5]

"The Dan Wheldon crash, I think, told everybody, 'Do you understand the dynamics of a motor racing accident? And, do you understand that interlocking wheels is what caused that?'" Stewart said in an interview with Chris Medland in 2012.

Stewart said the belated care he received after the wreck at Spa opened his eyes.

"I realized that if this was the best we had there was something sadly wrong: things wrong with the race track, the cars, the medical side, the fire fighting and the emergency crews."[6]

57

He Was Still Alive

ROGER WILLIAMSON WAS A 25-YEAR-OLD ENGLISH DRIVER WITH VAST potential when he took the green flag in the 1973 Dutch Grand Prix at Circuit Zandvoort early in his Formula One career.

Williamson had won the 1971 and 1972 Formula Three championships to gain a seat with the March Engineering team. The Dutch Grand Prix was his second race as a Formula One driver. On his eighth lap a tire failure caused his car to flip upside down and catch fire. Not seriously injured, Williamson nonetheless was trapped inside the burning, upside-down race car.

What happened then was one of the most heroic efforts ever made by a race driver on behalf of a peer. David Purley, a friend of Williamson's, stopped his car and raced to the burning vehicle, from which Williamson's cries for help could be heard. Frantically, Purley tried to turn the burning car back onto its wheels. Two track employees, untrained and without flame-retardant clothing, stood by as Purley struggled.

Purley then ran across the track in search of a fire extinguisher. Finding one in the possession of a track marshal he ran back and emptied it on the burning car, but the fire continued. Purley signaled for others to help, but none came, and it took eight minutes for the first fire truck to arrive at the scene.

The tragedy resulted in a rule change requiring fireproof clothing for all track-side marshals.[1]

58

Lower Leg Injuries Were Prevalent

WITH THE ADVENT OF THE REAR-ENGINE CAR CAME A RADICAL CHANGE in the way drivers were positioned within their open-cockpit cars. The most radical adjustment involved the almost prone position in which they were crouched in their seats with their feet well ahead of their torso. When a race car struck a wall, the feet became the first body part to feel the impact.

For a time a majority of racing injuries involved the feet. Limping race drivers became almost commonplace until engineers worked out a better way to soften the blows to the lower body.

One of the most horrifying accidents in recent years saw Alex Zanardi lose both of his legs in a 2001 crash in Germany. Zanardi started near the back of the field and was working his way forward. After a late pit stop Zanardi was preparing to merge back into traffic when his quick acceleration caused him to spin directly in the path of Patrick Carpentier, who avoided him. However, Alex Tagliano, who trailed Carpentier, plowed into the side of Zanardi's racer just in front of the steering wheel and sliced off the front of Zanardi's car.

The injured driver was flown to a Berlin hospital only a few miles away and nearly died after losing three-fourths of his blood supply.[1]

Zanardi never raced at Indianapolis because of the split between the two racing organizations, but he won the CART championship in 1997 and 1998.

Rick Mears won four Indianapolis 500s and, according to many, is the best driver who ever circumvented the Indianapolis Motor Speedway. One of his victories came after he had trailed by three laps around the 2.5-mile track.

But as good as Mears was on the ovals, serious foot injuries prevented him from doing well on the street and road courses. The quick and frequent braking was too difficult because of his foot injuries.

Mears spent a total of three months in several hospitals while surgeons performed skin grafts and worked to repair the broken bones. Mears said that when he woke up after the accident in Canada he looked down at his legs and saw that his feet were still attached. "I started to go unconscious again, but I did say to myself, 'You're going to drive again.'"[2]

The accident was at the Sanair track in the Molson Indy race on September 7, 1984. Mears's injuries slowed him for the remainder of his career. He won only two races the following two seasons.

From his rookie year in 1978 until 1992 Mears avoided hitting a wall at the Speedway. However, in 1992 he broke a wrist in a spectacular practice session accident and crashed out of the race for the first time. Later that year he announced his retirement at age 41.[3]

Alessandro Zampedri, an Italian who started three Indianapolis 500s, suffered extreme foot and leg injuries on the last lap of the 1996 race. Zampedri was running in fourth position as he entered the final turn of the race. Just ahead the cars of Roberto Guerrero and Eliseo Salazar came together and Zampedri's racer became airborne and spectacularly soared along the catch fencing before coming to a stop near the start-finish line.

Zampedri, who blamed Guerrero for the crash, returned to Indy in 1997 and later raced in Europe.

59

Flying Starts
Can Be Frightening

THE REPUTATION OF THE INDIANAPOLIS 500 ALWAYS HAS BEEN BUILT around the 33-car flying start. Eleven rows of tightly bunched race cars making it through the first turn is a high-risk proposition.

Fans who might not enjoy cars running in circles for three hours still are mesmerized by the start of the race. Some can't even stand to watch. Sending a man to the moon might be safer.

Mario Andretti said the standing start of a Formula One race may be as dangerous, but it's hard to match the thrill of 33 cars going into a 90-degree corner at well over 100 miles an hour.

Unlike in some types of racing, there is no warmup at the Indy 500. The first speed a driver feels all day is his most dangerous moment. Unlike Daytona, where the track is much wider and the high banks allow two or three cars to go through a corner comfortably, Indianapolis is narrow and basically flat. Drivers claim the corner looks even narrower when thousands of fans are close to the wall.

Almost every year there are rookies living the experience for the first time, although the veterans insist experience doesn't especially matter because there is no way to plan for what might happen. The emotions of the drivers are at a razor's edge, which can add danger, as it did in 1958.

When speeds were slower, the cars were more tightly bunched at the start, with the rows symmetrically in formation. As speeds increased considerably more space was allotted between rows, and hundreds of yards before the start drivers already were pulled out of formation hoping to find a seam toward a clear spot.

Even if all 33 cars make it safely through the first turn, the danger continues, at least until the cars become strung out. Unlike Daytona, the Speedway can only accommodate two cars going through a corner side by side. If three cars are even, at least one of them must peel off. The massive crashes in 1958 and 1964 might not have been so serious if the track had been wider.

One instance when all hell broke loose even before the first turn was the 1966 race when cars began spinning almost at the start-finish line. It started when Billy Foster, on the outside of the fourth row, nearly touched wheels with another car and spun into the outside wall. When the chaos ended, 14 cars had become involved.[1]

A. J. Foyt was the only casualty of the accident, scratching his hand climbing the catch fence on the outside of the track. Foyt, and others, obviously were concerned about the possibility of fire, but none occurred.

Eleven of the 14 were too torn up to resume racing, and following a lengthy cleanup the race was restarted with the cars in single file. Immediately after the green flag fell, Johnny Boyd crashed in the first turn.

The start of the 1973 race was equally dramatic and considerably more dangerous. Salt Walther, who started in the middle of the sixth row, was the principal casualty of the first-turn accident, but nine spectators also required hospitalization because of burning fuel spray.[2]

Tension may have been heightened by a four-hour delay in starting the race caused by rain that would continue to haunt the event.

Eleven cars were involved in the accident that was triggered by Walther's car touching wheels with Jerry Grant's. Salt's car struck the outside fence, severely damaging the fence and tearing off the front portion of the race car. Walther's vehicle turned over, was hit by other cars, and spun wildly toward the first turn with Walther's feet hanging out of its damaged front end.

Walther suffered severe burns among his injuries and was hospitalized for many weeks. Before the massive cleanup could be completed, the race was rained out.

The craziest accident at the start of a race occurred in 1982, even before the field had reached racing speeds. Kevin Cogan, starting in the middle of the first row, suddenly had his car turn sharply right and smash into Foyt's machine. Then it veered to the inside and took out the car of Mario Andretti. Cogan had managed to infuriate two of the Speedway's greatest icons in a matter of seconds.

Back in the field, 18-year-old rookie Dale Whittington lost control and took out both his car and that of Roger Mears. Cogan claimed he did nothing abnormal to make the car go right, but car owner Roger Penske never absolved him.

Foyt screamed at Cogan, and in a brief television interview lambasted "that damn Coogan." Asked what happened in a TV interview, Andretti said, "This is what happens when you have children doing a man's job up front."[3]

Race day in 1992 was one of the coldest on record, creating unsafe racing conditions that resulted in several accidents. The field hadn't even gotten to the green flag when pole-sitter Roberto Guerrero crashed.

Guerrero, a Colombian who finished fourth or higher in his first four 500s, was leading the field down the backstretch when his car suddenly lurched toward the infield and struck a guard rail. It was damaged enough that it was out of the race before it started.

The 33 drivers included four members of the Andretti family: Mario and sons Michael and Jeff and John Andretti, son of Mario's brother, Aldo. On lap 84 Mario crashed in the fourth turn, an accident blamed on cold tires. Andretti suffered broken toes. On the 115th lap Jeff Andretti hit the wall hard in the second turn and suffered extensive leg injuries that effectively ended his racing career. At the same time that his father and brother were being taken to Methodist Hospital, Michael Andretti was leading the race.

Michael dominated until the 186th lap when a broken fuel pump took him out of competition, setting up a photo finish in which Al Unser Jr. edged Scott Goodyear.[4]

Stan Fox's first-turn accident in the 1995 Indy 500 is difficult to erase from one's memory. An outstanding midget driver who was competing in his eighth 500, Fox was driving low on the track when he lost control and spun toward the outside wall. His car crashed hard into one driven by Eddie Cheever.

Cheever and Fox both rode along the outside wall with their cars heavily damaged. The often-shown video and still pictures reveal Fox's body protruding from the front of the race car.

Cheever avoided injuries, but Fox suffered serious head injuries that ended his career. Surprisingly, he had no broken bones nor any other significant injuries other than those to his head. Several other cars also were involved in the first-lap incident.

Fox continued to talk about making a comeback, but those close to him realized it would never happen. He was killed in December of 2000 in a head-on collision some 200 miles from Auckland, New Zealand. The 48-year-old Wisconsin native was driving at night en route to a meeting and collided with a truck and trailer unit.[5]

The 2001 Indy race saw Scott Sharp win the pole in his seventh of what would be 14 appearances in the 500. The veteran sports car driver spun out in the first turn of the race but all the trailing drivers avoided him.

60

Getting Out While Getting's Good

ART CROSS WAS A DRIVER DURING ONE OF AUTO RACING'S MOST DANGEROUS eras. Long before he died in 2005 at age 87 he had found the secret to living a long life.

It involved retiring from auto racing at age 37, before the sport had a good chance to claim him. He used the money he won from four Indy 500s to buy a farm near La Porte, Indiana, and his retirement lasted 50 years.

In 1952 Art Cross was the first Rookie of the Year at the Speedway, starting a still-standing tradition. He started 20th as a rookie and came in fifth. The next year he started eighth and was runner-up to winner Bill Vukovich. He finished 11th in 1954, finishing the 200 laps for the third straight year, and was 17th in 1955, when a rod broke after he had led 24 laps.

Cross won seven champ car races in four years, including three in 1954. He led a total of 202 laps among the 1,364 he ran during his short career.

During his last race Bill Vukovich was killed and Cal Niday seriously injured. After a final race at Milwaukee that year Cross decided to retire and spend time with his family. He already had faced enough danger, having been wounded in the Battle of the Bulge during World War II. After the war he returned to race midget cars; he later was inducted into the National Midget Auto Racing Hall of Fame.[1]

61

Major Survivable Crashes

MANY WHO WATCHED DALE EARNHARDT'S CRASH AT DAYTONA IN 2001 were surprised that the accident proved fatal. While the NASCAR icon unquestionable had a hard hit with the wall, there were other accidents that at first glance seemed more life threatening. Observers blamed the helmet Earnhardt was wearing, the way he was wearing it, and the way his seat belt was attached, among other things.

Since the arrival of such safety factors as the roll bar, the fire-retardant suit, the full-faced crash helmet, rubber fuel-tank liners, and, in later years, the HANS device (which supports the head and neck), there have been a number of accidents that in the past probably would have been fatal.

Two Indy car drivers, Mark Dismore and Kevin Cogan, survived high-speed crashes against concrete walls at the Indianapolis Motor Speedway. Dismore was practicing when his car veered sharply left toward the entrance of pit road. It rear-ended the fence and crossed the entrance to the pits and smashed at high speed into the barrier there. The car basically was ripped into two pieces, and Dismore suffered a broken neck.

Cogan escaped injury when his car struck three different walls near the entrance of pit road. The Californian brushed the outside wall as he came out of the fourth turn, and his car shot across the track and struck the inside pit wall heavily. The car rebounded against the barrier at the entrance of the pits, smashing a television camera that had recorded the violent impact. Cogan's car broke into pieces and slid along pit road on its side with Cogan still inside.

One of the most frightening accidents in Speedway history involved Hawaiian veteran Danny Ongais in the 1981 race. A look at the wrecked car, with Ongais clearly visible as it broke apart, suggested a likely fatality.

Ongais had led the race until a lingering pit stop on the 63rd lap. Upon leaving the pits he attempted to make a pass entering the third turn and the car's rear end drifted out toward the wall. When Ongais tried to correct the slide, his car crashed nearly head-on into the outer wall. The car's front end broke away, and Ongais, unconscious, rode it around the third-turn wall as oil burned around him.[1]

Probably more because of luck than safety measures he survived his injuries to race again.

Although he had driven in the 1983 Indy race, most of Patrick Bedard's previous experience was limited to writing about racing. Bedard, who was a writer for *Car and Driver* magazine, had enough experience to qualify for the 500 and started the 1984 race in the seventh row. Interviewed by John McGill of the *Louisville Courier-Journal,* Bedard said he didn't come to Indy to be killed.

But it's a wonder he wasn't.

On lap 58 his car tumbled through the infield near the fourth turn, breaking apart as the engine flew away. It slammed the inside wall and lay crumpled in wreckage. Bedard somehow survived with a concussion and broken jaw.

Bedard got a start in racing when *Car and Driver* ran a contest in the early 1970s challenging its readers to compete in a series of races it was sponsoring. Bedard finished first in a 1973 Chevy Vega GT, and nine years later was driving at Indy. He continued to write for *Car and Driver* until 2009.[2]

Tom Sneva's best days were still ahead of him in 1975, the year his car did a cartwheel through the second turn following contact with Eldon Rasmussen. The car was destroyed, but Sneva survived and went on to win the 500 in 1983 and finish second in 1977, 1978, and 1980.

Sneva was a well-spoken, well-educated, and sometimes outspoken driver who sometimes crossed opinions with his peers and mechanics. Fellow driver Gordon Johncock once said, "If nine people pushed the up button in the elevator, Sneva would push down."[3]

62

No Chance of Survival

SOME RACING ACCIDENTS ARE SO VIOLENT, SO OVERWHELMING IN SCOPE, that the driver is doomed no matter what safety devices are involved. Every race driver realizes he may be victimized by such an incident and weighs the odds of it happening.

Justin Wilson, an extremely likeable British driver who died in such an accident at Pocono Raceway in 2015, undoubtedly considered such odds, but he never would have expected the fluke type of accident that took his life. When race leader Sage Karam crashed, the heavy nose cone of his car broke free and flew down the track. Wilson, who was several hundred yards behind Karam, was struck in the head by the giant piece of debris.

Wilson was knocked unconscious and his car came to rest on the inside part of the track. He died the following day. The 37-year-old driver was competing in the IndyCar Series, having previously driven in Formula One and the Champ Car series. Wilson was married and the father of two daughters.

NASCAR driver Tony Stewart loaned his private plane to the Wilson family so they could fly to the Pennsylvania track.[1]

Close wheel-to-wheel racing, an earmark of the IndyCar Series in recent years, cost the sport one of its most popular drivers in a massive, multi-car accident at Las Vegas in 2011.

Two-time Indianapolis 500 winner Dan Wheldon died after the 15-car crash on the 11th lap. The accident was visible on live television and possibly was the most horrifying wreck seen in America's homes. After starting at the rear of the field, the 33-year-old Wheldon was working his way through the traffic when cars began flying all over the track. The network had a camera in Wheldon's car that showed the initial stages of the accident. Wheldon's car became airborne and sailed into the catch fence above the outer wall. The fence is designed to protect spectators from flying debris or out-of-control race cars.

Fellow driver Ryan Briscoe described the track as a "war zone," with pieces of metal everywhere and cars on fire. Videos seemed to show that Wade Cunningham's car swerved and J. R. Hildebrand drove over the left rear tire of Cunningham's car.

The scene was one of the most emotional ever seen at a racing tragedy. Dario Franchitti was among many visibly crying. The race was canceled, and the undamaged cars were lined up for a five-lap, low-speed tribute to the defending Indy champion.

Drivers had expressed concern about the high speeds at the track, which reached more than 220 mph.

"We all had a bad feeling about this place in particular, just because of the high banking and how easy it was to go flat [top speed]," driver Oriol Servia said. "If you give us the opportunity, we are drivers and we try to go to the front. We knew it could happen."[2]

Three other drivers suffered lesser injuries in the race.

The ultra-popular Wheldon left a wife and two sons.

When racing people refer to a head-on collision with a wall they often think about Gordon Smiley, whose clash with the third-turn wall at the Speedway may have been the hardest hit ever.

The first hour of qualifying on May 15, 1982, saw multiple speed records set, and Smiley left the pits for his qualification run with a good 10-mile run as his goal. But on a practice lap the rear of his car veered right entering the third turn. Smiley appeared to attempt a correction but the car went straight into the concrete, disintegrating in a wall of fire and debris. The 33-year-old veteran of two Indy races died instantly.

A. J. Foyt said after the accident that he felt Indy cars had been made safer because of recently adopted ground effects, which increase the downforce on a car.

"I think the cars are safe, until you hit wrong," Foyt said. "If you hit just wrong I don't care if it's a Sherman tank. It's all over."[3]

Greg Moore may have been one of the best drivers never to race in the Indianapolis 500. The Canadian driver won the Indy Lights championship at age 20 and ran 72 races in the Champ Car series over a four-year period prior to his death in 1999 at age 24.

Moore started the 1999 season with a win at Homestead, Florida, his fifth victory in the CART series. Moore was to drive the 2000 season for Roger Penske, a sign that he was among the top drivers in his sport. However, in the final race of the season at California Speedway Moore was killed in a one-car accident.

That day's Marlboro 500 was to decide the season's driving championship between Juan Pablo Montoya and Dario Franchitti. Shortly before the race Moore was knocked off his motor scooter by another vehicle and injured his hand. Doubts arose over whether he would be able to drive in the race, but he was cleared by medics on the condition that he wear a hand brace.[4] On the ninth lap of the race Moore lost control in the second turn, and the car entered the infield grass at more than 200 miles an hour. It hit an access road, overturned, and hit a concrete wall in the infield with the top of the car directly hitting the wall. Moore's body was crushed between the car and the wall. The ride Penske had designated for Moore was given to Helio Castroneves, who won the Indy 500 three times for Penske.

63

Bill Cheesbourg,
One of a Kind

LONG AFTER MANY OF HIS COMPETITORS WERE DEAD OR RETIRED, Arizona native Bill Cheesbourg was driving race cars. Although his champ car days were over, Cheesbourg was racing stock cars at local tracks around Tucson and even competed in figure-eight races for fun. In the mid-70s Cheesbourg won a NASCAR Grand National West race in Phoenix, and he raced until the early '80s.

Cheesbourg, who died in 1995 at age 68, competed in six races at Indianapolis, with a best finish of 10th in 1958. Otherwise, success was hard to come by at the Speedway, where he started 33rd, or last, three times. One of those was the '58 race, but he was far enough behind the accident to avoid it.

Cheesbourg had one of the longest careers in racing, beginning with a Soap Box Derby race at age 11. That was a bit of a disaster, because his wheels, lacking ball bearings and taken from his little red wagon, came off soon after the start. But Bill Cheesbourg was a hard guy to keep down, and the next year he won the race.

Already bitten by the racing bug, Cheesbourg assembled a 1932 Ford coupe and in 1955 earned $28,000 racing it. He said he raced it three nights a week and even ran it in a 24-hour marathon race.[1]

Cheesbourg had a ride in the popular Novi in 1958, and that was the only time he finished the 500. He started 33rd in the fire-marked 1964 race and again got through the trouble to finish 16th.

64

Sutton Retired after Seeing Kenyon Wreck

MANY OF THE 1958 DRIVERS WHO AVOIDED DISASTER ON THE RACETRACK lived long and fruitful lives. They included Don Freeland, who lived until age 82; Johnny Boyd, 77; Jim Rathmann, 83; Bob Christie, 85; Mike Magill, 86; and Len Sutton, 81.

Sutton, perhaps the best driver to come out of Oregon, was a rookie in the 1958 Indianapolis 500 and was knocked out of competition in the third-turn accident. The massive crash sidelined four rookies: Paul Goldsmith, Jerry Unser, Art Bisch, and Sutton.

After his release from the navy in 1946 Sutton quickly displayed his potential at tracks around Portland and Salem. He won so many races in the Northwest that he left the area in 1956 to run at a higher level. He posted three wins in champ cars in 76 career starts and drove in five Indy 500s, finishing second to teammate Rodger Ward in 1962. Sutton retired in 1965 after a race at the dangerous Langhorne track in Pennsylvania.

"We had a real bad accident, a midget driver whose name is Mel Kenyon, got severely burned," Sutton once told Bill Poehler of the *Salem Statesman Journal*. "I got out of the car that day and said to myself, 'I think my family's too important. I've got to hang it up.'"[1]

While Sutton decided to hang it up, the man involved in the horrible accident decided to keep racing. To do so, Kenyon somehow would need to replace almost all the fingers on his left hand.

His engine blew up at Langhorne, spilling oil on his fire suit and the track. Kenyon's car spun, hit a wall, and knocked the driver unconscious.

"He would have died but Joe Leonard stopped his car and jumped out. Two fans jumped over the fence and pulled Mel out of his car and saved his life," said Robin Miller of *Racer* magazine.[2]

Kenyon went through numerous operations at the US Army Burn Center in San Antonio. His brother and father designed a special glove that fit on his hand and hooked to the steering wheel. Kenyon returned to racing the next year and recorded a dozen first- or second-place finishes. Eleven months after his accident he qualified for the Indianapolis 500 and finished fifth, one of his four top-five finishes at Indy.

In 1967 Kenyon won 17 of the 49 midget feature races in which he competed. He won more than 100 midget races in 1984 and continued racing after his 70th birthday in 2003.

"If you were fast in a midget or a sprint car back in the early '50s, you were going to get a chance in the Indy 500," Miller said.[3]

65

Boyd Saw a Lot of Action

JOHNNY BOYD WAS FROM FRESNO, CALIFORNIA, ALSO THE HOMETOWN of two-time Indy winner Bill Vukovich. Both were involved in one of the most famous crashes in Speedway history, but Boyd was lucky and Vukovich was not.

Boyd made 56 starts in champ car races between 1954 and 1966, finishing in the top 10 31 times. Before arriving in Indianapolis Boyd became close friends with Bob Sweikert, who would win the 1955 race and be killed at Salem (Indiana) Speedway the next year.

Boyd was a Speedway rookie in '55, and Sweikert helped him overcome handling problems before the race.[1] Boyd then qualified in the next-to-last row. While leading the race Vukovich crashed on the backstretch when the track became blocked, and he ran over the top of Boyd's car, crashing to his death and leaving Boyd's car upside down. Driver Al Keller and Speedway marshals upended Boyd, who suffered only friction burns.

Johnny Boyd went on to race in 12 Indianapolis races, with his best finish a third after avoiding the first-lap mishap in 1958. He recorded five top-10 finishes and retired after the 1966 race in which a first-turn crash eliminated 11 starters. Boyd was in the crash but was awarded 22nd place, ahead of the other eliminated cars.[2]

Johnny died in 2003 at age 77.

66

Speed and Safety
May Not Mix

ENGINEERS WHO BUILD INDY CARS ARE CHALLENGED ON TWO CON-
flicting fronts. Drivers want their race cars to be as safe as possible. Car owners, while also concerned about safety, want them built to go fast enough to
win races.

Until the 1990s, engineers were doing amazing things in terms of speed.
Pole day sometimes saw the track record broken three times within a few hours.
Since the Speedway first opened in 1909, cars kept going faster until qualifying
speeds finally topped out at 237.498 miles an hour.

Arie Luyendyk, a two-time winner, set the standard in 1990, but speeds fell
off when the Indy Racing League changed car specifications in 1997. No one
has approached Luyendyk's record since.

The new IRL-sanctioned machines went slower but for a time had safety
issues. Davy Jones, runner-up in the 1996 race, suffered serious back injuries
that year, and cars backing into walls was a serious issue for a time.

Even with slower speeds, the IRL races were hair-raising because cars often
ran only inches apart. Occasionally the tires touched and sometimes horrible
accidents occurred, such as the Dan Wheldon accident in Los Angeles. Ironi-
cally, Wheldon had done significant testing of a new chassis that would be adopted by Indy cars the year after his death.[1]

The sleeker new car revised the concept of open-wheel racing, which had
been the exclusive type of Indy racing forever. The rear wheels of the new

model sit partially enclosed, which makes touching wheels less likely. The front wheels aren't as enclosed as the rear but still provide some protection. The driver now sits eight inches farther back in the cockpit, and the space around him is longer, wider, and encased with high-impact foam.

After running the tests, Wheldon estimated the new car would be 30 percent safer than its predecessor.

IndyCar Series officials are constantly looking for new safety devices. One that remains controversial involves a tether attached to the nose cone to prevent it from flying off the car and striking someone, as it did in the accident that killed Justin Wilson.

"There's been some renderings of almost like a boomerang-looking device in front of the driver that wouldn't block the vision but would deflect something like this," driver Ryan Hunter-Reay said.

Putting a canopy over the cockpit is another possible safety device that drivers debate. Indy car racing always has been the open-cockpit kind.

Former 500 winner Eddie Cheever questions if a canopy is a good idea, telling Bob Pockrass of ESPN.com, "I'd hate to be in one of those canopies and it doesn't open and the car catches on fire. Nothing is that simple in racing."[2]

"Every accident is different," Mario Andretti told Pockrass. "Whether it's NASCAR, whether it's any form of the sport, you always learn something."

Race car designer Nigel Bennett once said, "For a driver to survive an accident at that kind of speed, it involves a certain amount of luck. A head-on crash at anything much above 50 miles an hour is unsurvivable. The human body just won't survive that sort of deceleration. The internal organs get irreparably damaged.[3]

Unlimited hydroplane racing, which in the past has seen several drivers killed by crashes on the water, has become safer by using capsules. The sport lost two of its icons in the early '80s when Bill Muncey died in a blow-over at Acapulco, Mexico. Nine months later Dean Chenoweth died in a similar accident near Tri-Cities, Washington. Those accidents led to unlimited hydroplanes adopting canopies, and the sport hasn't had a fatality since.[4]

Almost any implementation in the name of safety has a second side. Rex Mays, a giant of the 1940s, thought seat belts could be hazardous. If he had worn one on November 6, 1949, he would have survived to race again.

As Mario Andretti said, he could look around the room at a drivers' meeting and wonder who would be missing at the end of the season.[5]

NOTES

1. A CONVOLUTED ACCOUNT OF THE CRASH

1. Transcript, Indianapolis Motor Speedway's Radio Network, May 30, 1958.

2. A RACE-DAY SHOOTOUT

1. Donald Davidson, *The Talk of Gasoline Alley,* May 2, 2012, WFNI-1070.
2. "Indiana Horse Trainer Held in Love Triangle Shooting," *Nashua Telegraph,* June 1, 1976.

3. MAY WAS BUSTING OUT ALL OVER

1. Bill Marvel, interview by author, September 23, 2016.
2. *Indianapolis Star,* May 31, 1958.
3. Joe Scalzo, *Indianapolis Roadsters, 1952–1964* (Osceola, WI: Motorbooks, 1999).
4. A. J. Foyt and William Neely, *A. J.* (New York: Times Books, 1983), 77.
5. *Indianapolis Star,* May 31, 1958.

4. O'CONNOR'S ETERNAL HOME

1. Jeff O'Connor, interview by author, September 15, 2016.
2. Bryce Mayer, interview by author, September 15, 2016.
3. O'Connor, interview.
4. Bruce Mayer, "NV Legend Memorialized," *North Vernon Plain Dealer & Sun,* August 20, 2015, 12A.
5. Mayer, interview.
6. Lendal Patterson, interview by author, September 20, 2016.
7. Bill Marvel, interview by author, September 23, 2016.

5. THE CITY OF RAILROADS

1. Bryce Mayer, interview by author, September 15, 2016.
2. "History," City of North Vernon, Indiana, *NorthVernon-in.gov.*
3. Ibid.
4. All quotations of Jeff O'Connor are from an interview by the author, September 15, 2016.

6. DEADLY SUMMER OF '58

1. *Deadliest Crash: The Le Mans 1955 Disaster,* BBC Four documentaries, broadcast May 16, 2010.
2. Steve Zautke, "Art Bisch Thrilled the Milwaukee Fans in 1958," *RacingNation.com,* December 4, 2010.
3. "Race Driver Jimmy Reece Dies in Crash," *Chicago Daily Tribune,* September 29, 1958, 3.
4. Bill Marvel, interview by author, September 23, 2016.

7. SAFETY WASN'T FIRST

1. Michael J. Kollins, Motorsports Hall of Fame of America.
2. "Two Perished in Auto Race," *Evening Citizen* (Ottawa), August 20, 1909.
3. "Bruce Keene & Wrecked Marmon," *FirstSuperSpeedway.com; Wikipedia,* s.v. "List of Fatalities at the Indianapolis Motor Speedway."
4. "Death Claims Further Toll," *Evening Sentinel* (Rochester, IN), August 23, 1909.
5. Donald Davidson, *The Talk of Gasoline Alley,* June 15, 2005, WIBC-1070.

8. DAYTONA ENTERS THE PICTURE

1. "George Amick Dies in 170 m.p.h. Crash," *Chicago Sunday Tribune,* April 5, 1959.
2. National Midget Auto Racing Hall of Fame, press release, 2009.
3. Bob Gates, "George Amick's Tragic Daytona Race," *National Speed Sport News,* November 20, 2014.

9. NO AVERAGE DAY AT THE BEACH

1. "History of NASCAR," *Hometracks.Nascar.com,* August 17, 2010.
2. "Marshall Teague," *MarshallTeague.com,* February 15, 2013.
3. "Just Playing Around at 171 mph—Teague," *Daytona Beach Morning Journal,* February 10, 1959.
4. "Teague Dies in Daytona Wreck," *Spartanburg Herald,* February 12, 1959.

10. CHAMPION OF THE DIRT

1. "Jimmy Bryan Indianapolis 500 Stats," *Indy500.com*, May 2006.

11. HOW FAST IS TOO FAST?

1. Corky Simpson, "Racer Bill Cheesbourg Lived His Whole Life as a Winner," *Tucson Citizen*, November 7, 1995.
2. *Wikipedia*, s.v. "Race of Two Worlds."
3. Graham Gauld, "Question," *Ecurie Ecosse*, June 26, 2008.
4. *Wikipedia*, s.v. "Race of Two Worlds."
5. Sam S. Collins and Gavin D. Ireland, *Autodrome: The Lost Race Circuits of Europe* (Poundbury, UK: Veloce, 2005).

12. O'CONNOR VICTIM OF JINX?

1. *Sports Illustrated*, November 9, 2011.

13. JERRY UNSER, UNLUCKY TRENDSETTER

1. William Eggert, "Jerry Unser, Burned in Crash, Is Dead," *Indianapolis Star*, May 18, 1959.
2. "Jerry Unser Jr.," *UnserRacingMuseum.com*.
3. Bill Marvel, interview by author, September 23, 2016.
4. "Bobby Unser," *UnserRacingMuseum.com*.
5. "Al Unser Jr.," *UnserRacingMuseum.com*.

14. THE GOOD AND BAD OF ED ELISIAN

1. "Ed Elisian Involved in Fatal Crash Again," *Milwaukee Journal*, June 30, 1958.
2. "Sweikert Killed in Race Crash," *Kentucky New Era* (Hopkinsville, KY), June 18, 1956.
3. Bill Marvel, interview by author, September 23, 2016.
4. Rick Johnson, "Elisian: I Thought There Was Enough Room," *Indianapolis Times*, May 31, 1958.
5. Ibid.
6. Joe Scalzo, *Indianapolis Roadsters, 1952–1964* (Osceola, WI: Motorbooks, 1999).
7. Marvel, interview by author.

15. JOURNEYMEN DRIVERS ALSO VICTIMIZED

1. "Dick Linder Dies in Crash," *Pittsburgh Post-Gazette*, April 20, 1959.
2. "Gamble Proves Costly, Randall Killed in Crash," *Reading Eagle* (Reading, PA), July 2, 1962.

3. "Van Johnson Dies in 'Jinx' Racing Car," *Pittsburgh Press,* July 20, 1959.

4. Dale Burgess, "Bob Cortner Dies of Head Injuries Suffered in Indianapolis Practice Run," *Youngstown Vindicator,* May 20, 1959.

16. DEATH COMMON AT LANGHORNE

1. "Historical Marker Search," *Pennsylvania Historical and Museum Commission,* Commonwealth of Pennsylvania, web.

2. Preston Lehner, "The Legend of Puke Hollow: Remembering Langhorne Speedway," *Motor Trend,* April 22, 1914.

3. Ron Hedger, "The King of Langhorne," *Stock Car Racing* 35, no. 2 (February 2000).

4. Riggs, *Langhorne! No Man's Land* (Zionsville, IN: Pitstop, 2008).

5. Hedger, "The King of Langhorne."

6. *National Speed Sport News,* May 11, 2010.

7. Lehner, "The Legend of Puke Hollow."

8. Ibid.

17. THE SHORT CAREER OF BOBBY BALL

1. Bob Gates, "Bobby Ball Could Have Been One of America's Greats," *SpeedSport .com,* March 2, 2010.

18. SPEEDWAY CLAIMS BETTENHAUSEN

1. "Fatalities, Tony Bettenhausen," Indianapolis Motor Speedway press release, May 1961.

2. Ibid.

3. Ibid.

4. Ibid.

19. TONY'S LEGACY CONTINUES

1. Milton Richmond, "One Armed Bettenhausen Making Comeback," *Willimantic Chronicle,* August 30, 1973.

2. Paul Reinhard, "Driver Gary Bettenhausen Dies at 72," *Chicago Tribune,* March 17, 2014.

3. Ibid.

4. Jack Thompson, "Bettenhausen, Wife, 2 Others Die in Plane Crash," *Chicago Tribune,* February 15, 2000.

20. CHECK OUT THOSE HELMETS

1. Donald Simpson, "Helmets in Surgical History," *Australia and New Zealand Journal of Surgery* 66, no. 5: 314–24.

2. O. Minoyama and H. Tsuchida, "Injuries in Professional Motor Car Racing at a Racing Circuit between 1996 and 2000," *Journal of Sports Medicine* 38, no. 5: 613–16.

3. Mark Aumann, "Safety Improvements, Changes Define Racing Eras," *Nascar .com*, February 16, 2011.

21. KELLER IN VUKOVICH CRASH

1. *Wikipedia*, s.v. "Alvah Keller."

2. Shav Glick, "Rodger Ward, 83; Oldest Living Winner of Indianapolis 500," *Los Angeles Times*, July 6, 2004.

3. Lisette Hilton, "Vukovich Was a Fearless Racing Legend," *ESPN.com*, http:// www.espn.com/classic/biography/s/Vukovich_Bill.html.

22. THOMSON KNOWN FOR BRAVERY

1. Biography at National Midget Auto Racing Hall of Fame.

2. "Johnny Thomson Killed in Crash at Allentown," *Indianapolis Star*, September 25, 1960.

23. AMONG ALL ELSE, FOYT IS SURVIVOR

1. Dave Kallmann, "A. J. Foyt Returns to Road America, Reminisces," *USA Today*, June 25, 2016.

2. Robert Markus, "Elkhart Lake Crash Perils Foyt's Career," *Chicago Tribune*, September 24, 1990.

3. "Indianapolis Motor Speedway: The House That A. J. Foyt Built," *Autoweek*, April 8, 2016.

24. SACHS ALMOST WON IN '61

1. "A. J. Foyt Wins '500' in Frantic Finish Battle with Eddie Sachs," *Indianapolis Star*, May 31, 1961.

2. Ibid.

25. THE LITTLE CAR THAT COULD

1. "Fist Fight Breaks Out between Speedway Winner Parnelli Jones and Eddie Sachs," *Lewiston Daily Sun*, June 1, 1963.

26. EVERYONE LOVED THE NOVI

1. Clint Brawner and Joe Scalzo, *Indy 500 Mechanic: The Inside Story of Big Time Auto Racing* (Radnor, PA: Chilton, 1975).

2. "Duke Nalon Tamed Powerful Novi Like No Other Driver," *Motorsport.com*, May 8, 2000.

27. INNOCENT VICTIMS

1. "Bettenhausen Tire Flies into Stands, Killing Spectator," *Los Angeles Times*, May 25, 1987.
2. Shav Glick, "Three Spectators Die at US 500," *Los Angeles Times*, July 27, 1998.
3. Bill Fleischman, "Tragedy in Charlotte Is Felt All Over," *Philly.com*, May 4, 1999.
4. "3 Fans Killed at Indy Race," *CBSNews.com*, May 1, 1999.

28. SPORT LOSES TWO GOOD MEN

1. Art Garner, *Black Noon* (Griffin, 2016).
2. *1985 Indianapolis 500 Media Fact Book,* compiled by Bill Donaldson and Bob Laycock.
3. Garner, *Black Noon.*
4. Henri Greuter, "The Indy 1964 Second-Lap Disaster: Closing in on the Truth," Part 3: May 30, 1964, *8w.forix.com*, October 25, 2010.
5. "Eddie Sachs," *MotorsportsMemorial.org.*
6. "Bobby Marshman Burned as Auto Crashes into Wall," *St. Petersburg Times*, November 28, 1964.
7. "Bobby Marshman Critical Today," *Gettysburg Times*, November 30, 1964.
8. "Race Driver Bobby Marshman Dies," *Prescott Evening Courier*, December 5, 1964.
9. *Wikipedia*, s.v. "Dave MacDonald," last modified August 31, 2016.

29. HE WAS A WONDERFUL GENTLEMAN

1. Jani Lange, "Sid Collins," *Indiana Journalism Hall of Fame*, mediaschool.indiana.edu/ijhf/.
2. Mike Larson, "#16 Sid Collins' Impromptu Eulogy of Eddie Sachs Touches Racing Fans," *Autoweek.com*, May 13, 2016.

30. FIRE AND FEAR ARE SYNONYMOUS

1. Kim Chapin, "The Ghost of Indy's Past," *Sports Illustrated*, May 15, 1978.
2. *1981 Indianapolis Motor Speedway: Day-by-Day Trackside Report, Indy500.com.*
3. Super Marauder, "Glenn 'Fireball' Roberts: Biography," *IMDb.com.*
4. "Niki Lauda Badly Injured in German Grand Prix," *Guardian*, August 2, 1976.

31. JUST GET IT OVER

1. Phil Richards, "Deadly May of 1973 Still Resonates at Indianapolis Motor Speedway," *USA Today,* May 21, 2013.
2. Ibid.
3. Jim Slocum, "Johncock Wins Shortened 500," *Milwaukee Sentinel,* May 31, 2013.

32. DANGER HIGHEST ON SHORT TRACKS

1. Gary Schwab, Alexander Amess, and David Scott, "More Than 520 people Have Died in U.S. Auto Racing in Past 25 Years," *Charlotte Observer,* August 16, 2014.

33. '58 DRIVERS CAN'T ESCAPE FATE

1. Donald Davidson, *The Talk of Gasoline Alley,* May 2, 2014, WFNI-1070.
2. Biography at the National Midget Auto Racing Hall of Fame.
3. Joe Scalzo, *Indianapolis Roadsters: 1952–1964* (Osceola, WI: Motorbooks, 1999).

34. DODGE LOSES IN PHOTO FINISH

1. Donald Davidson, *The Talk of Gasoline Alley,* May 11, 2010, WFNI-1070.
2. "The 1971 Challenger Pace Car Crash at the Indianapolis 500," *The 1970 Hamtramck Registry,* http://www.hamtramck-historical.com/.

35. PHRASE ALMOST PROPHETIC

1. Jim Murray and Linda McCoy Murray, *Quotable Jim Murray: The Literary Wit, Wisdom, and Wonder of a Distinguished American Sports Columnist* (Nashville, TN: Towlehouse, 2003).

36. LATER THAT NIGHT HE WAS GONE

1. Lars Anderson, "Life and Death and the Heart of American Racing," *Sports Illustrated,* May 25, 2013.
2. Bill Marvel, interview by author, September 23, 2016.

37. JUD LARSON, A BREED APART

1. Joe Scalzo, *Indianapolis Roadsters, 1952–1964* (Osceola, WI: Motorbooks, 1999).
2. "Reading, PA Race Drivers Killed," *GenDisasters.com,* June 1966.
3. "Jud Larson Indianapolis 500 Stats," *IndianapolisMotorSpeedway.com.*

38. A NEW RIVAL FOR INDY

1. Darrell Waltrip, interview by author.
2. Cale Yarborough and William Neely, *Cale: The Life and Times of America's Greatest Stock Car Driver* (New York: Times Books, 1986).
3. Stan Sutton, *Sporting News*, June 30, 1986.

39. WARD'S TIME FINALLY ARRIVES

1. Robin Miller, "Robin Miller on Rodger Ward," video, *Racer.com*, February 16, 2016, www.racer.com/indycar/item/126166-racer-video-robin-miller-on-rodger -ward.
2. Donald Davidson, *The Talk of Gasoline Alley*, WFNI-1070, May 3, 2010.
3. Donald Davidson, *The Talk of Gasoline Alley*, WIBC-1070, May 9, 2007.

40. DICK IS JIM AND JIM IS DICK

1. "Jim Rathmann Indianapolis 500 Stats," *IndianapolisMotorSpeedway.com*.
2. Donald Davidson, *The Talk of Gasoline Alley*, WFNI-1070, May 11, 2011.
3. John Nelson, "The AstroVette," *SuperChevy.com*, June 2009.

41. WARD WALKS AWAY

1. Richard Goldstein, "Rodger Ward, 83, Two-Time Indianapolis Winner," *New York Times*, July 7, 2004.
2. Ibid.

42. MAJOR CELEBRITIES MISSED RACE

1. "About Us," *Shelby.com*.
2. Shav Glick and Jerry Hirsch, "Carroll Shelby Dies at 89: Cult Classic Car Designer," *Los Angeles Times*, May 12, 2012.
3. Dean Ricci, "Cobra—The Living Legend," last updated September 18, 2015, www.deanricci.com/mcr/mag/slol/1999/cobralegend/.
4. Ibid.
5. "Drivers: Juan-Manuel Fangio," *Grandprix.com*.
6. Ibid.
7. "1956 Indy 500 Winner Pat Flaherty Dies at 76," *Autoweek*, April 9, 2002.
8. Shav Glick, Motorsports Hall of Fame of America, press release, 2005.
9. Ibid.
10. Robin Miller, "Robin Miller on Indy 500 Winner Troy Ruttman," video, *Racer.com*, http://www.racer.com/indycar/item/124715-racer-video-robin-miller -on-indy-500-winner-troy-ruttman.

11. "3-Time Indianapolis 500 Racer Eddie Russo Dies at 86," *AutoWeek*, October 22, 2012.

12. "22-Year-Old Ruttman Is Youngest Indy 500 Winner," *Indianapolis Star*, May 31, 1952.

43. DICK, THE OTHER RATHMANN

1. "Pat O'Connor Fatal Crash, 'All Known Angles,'" YouTube video, 2:03, posted by RacingAccidents3, December 14, 2013, https://www.youtube.com/watch?v=Ilk CpItEpzM.

2. "Winner of 1960 Indianapolis 500 Dies at 83," *Los Angeles Times*, November 25, 2011.

3. "Wheeling, Dealing for Final Spot in Indy 500 Is Under Way," *St. Joseph (MO) Gazette*, May 24, 1984.

44. HOLLYWOOD COMES TO INDY

1. Donald Davidson, "Beauty and the Brickyard," 2004 Indianapolis 500 program, 142.

2. Ibid.

45. FANS FALL TO THEIR DEATH

1. Donald Davidson, *The Talk of Gasoline Alley*, WIBC-1070, May 22, 2000; *Wikipedia*, s.v. "1960 Indianapolis 500."

46. GOLDSMITH WAS MULTI-DIMENSIONAL

1. Robin Miller, "Robin Miller on Paul Goldsmith," video, 4:11, *Racer.com*, November 23, 2015, http://www.racer.com/indycar/item/123936-racer-video-robin-miller-on-paul-goldsmith.

2. "Paul Goldsmith," *AMA Motorcycle Hall of Fame*, http://www.motorcycle museum.org/halloffame/detail.aspx?RacerID=26.

3. Ibid.

47. THE LADY LOST HER LIFE

1. "Biography of Janet Guthrie," *JanetGuthrie.com.*

2. John Geis, "Crash Kills Woman Racing at El Cajon," *Los Angeles Times*, October 7, 1991.

48. INDY AMONG TOP-10 DANGEROUS TRACKS

1. Jeff, "Top 10 Deadliest Racetracks in the World," *TheRichest.com*, February 20, 2014.

49. THE FORMER WINNER'S LAST RACE

1. Donald Davidson, "Johnnie Parsons," *Motorsports Hall of Fame of America,* http://www.mshf.com/hall-of-fame/inductees/johnnie-parsons.html.

50. DEATH WASN'T ONLY BAD RESULT

1. "Courageous Former Driver Bob Hurt Dies at 61," *Motorsport.com,* September 28, 2000.

2. "Sam Schmidt," *Schmidt Peterson Motorsports,* http://spm.ahutson.com /owners/.

3. "Tragedy Hits Sam Schmidt Hard," *ESPN.com,* October 17, 2011.

52. MARIO SURVIVES SPECTACULAR FLIP

1. Dave Colabro, *WTHR Evening News,* April 23, 2000.

53. THE MOST DEADLY SPORT?

1. "Mangled Horses, Maimed Jockeys," *New York Times,* March 24, 2012; "Horse Racing: America's Most Dangerous Game?" *Fresh Air,* National Public Radio, May 9, 2012.

2. John Schell and AAP, "Being a Jockey: The Most Dangerous Job on Land," *Sydney Morning Herald,* January 19, 2009.

54. THE TRIALS OF CAL NIDAY

1. Terry Reed, *Indy: The Race and Ritual of the Indianapolis 500* (Washington, DC: Potomac Books, 2005).

55. WEYANT, THE OLDEST SURVIVOR

1. *One on One with Mark Montieth,* WFNI-1070, May 13, 2012; Donald Davidson, *The Talk of Gasoline Alley,* WFNI-1070, May 18, 2015.

2. Marcia Martinez, "Oldest Living Indy 500 Driver Reflects on Memorable Life," *State Journal-Register* (Peoria, IL), May 29, 2011.

3. "Chuck Weyant," biography at National Midget Auto Racing Hall of Fame.

4. Martinez, "Oldest Living Indy 500 Driver."

56. STEWART PUSHES FOR SAFETY

1. Tom Rubython, "Turbo Charged by Lust: How Formula 1 Womaniser James Hunt Slept with 33 BA Air Stewardesses before Race," *DailyMail.com,* October 14, 2010.

2. Gerald Donaldson, "Jackie Stewart," *Formula1.com,* https://www.formula1 .com/en/championship/drivers/hall-of-fame/Jackie_Stewart.html.

3. The official website of Sir Jackie Stewart, www.sirjackiestewart.com.

4. Ibid.

5. Chris Medland, "Safety First," *ESPN.com,* January 11, 2012.

6. "Jackie Stewart Quotes," *BrainyQuotes.com.*

57. HE WAS STILL ALIVE

1. Mark Haggan, "The Tragic Death of Roger Williamson and the Heroism of David Purley," *MarkHaggan.com,* March 19, 2013.

58. LOWER LEG INJURIES WERE PREVALENT

1. Tom Cary, "Alex Zanardi Puts Life Threatening Champ Car Crash behind Him to Go for Gold in Hand Cycling at London," *Telegraph,* December 23, 2011.

2. "Rick Mears, on the Road to Recovery after Sept. 7 Crash, Is Testing Cars," *Los Angeles Times,* July 14, 1985.

3. Gordon Kirby, *Rick Mears, Thanks: The Story of Rick Mears and the Mears Gang* (East Sussex, UK: Crash Media Group, 2008).

59. FLYING STARTS CAN BE FRIGHTENING

1. Mark Bissett, "Graham Hill's 'American Red Ball Spl' Lola T90 Ford: Indy Winner 1966," *Primotipo.com,* June 12, 2015, https://primotipo.com/2015/06/12 /graham-hills-american-red-ball-spl-lola-t90-ford-indy-winner-1966–2/.

2. "The Race That's Difficult to Erase," *Times Daily,* May 26, 1988.

3. 1982 Indianapolis 500 television broadcast, ABC Sports, May 30, 1982.

4. 1992 Indianapolis 500 television broadcast, ABC Sports, May 24, 1992. Available in entirety on YouTube as "1992 Indianapolis 500."

5. "Stan Fox Dies in Car Crash," *MRN.com,* December 21, 2000, http://www .mrn.com/Race-Series/World-of-Outlaws/News/Articles/2000/12/Stan-Fox-Dies -In-Car-Crash.aspx.

60. GETTING OUT WHILE GETTING'S GOOD

1. Biography at National Midget Auto Racing Hall of Fame, archived September 27, 2007, at the Wayback Machine.

61. MAJOR SURVIVABLE CRASHES

1. John McGill, "Andretti, Johncock, and Foyt File Protest," *Louisville Courier-Journal,* May 25, 1981.

2. John McGill, "Curiosity and a Racer's Heart Drew Pat Bedard to Indy," *Louisville Courier-Journal*, May 17, 1981.

3. Robin Miller, "Tom Sneva," *Motorsports Hall of Fame of America*, http://www.mshf.com/hall-of-fame/inductees/tom-sneva.html.

62. NO CHANCE OF SURVIVAL

1. Jordan Bianchi, "Tony Stewart Sends Plane to Fly Family of Injured IndyCar Driver Justin Wilson," *SBNation.com*, August 24, 2015.

2. John Marshall, "Indy 500 Winner Wheldon Dies After Massive Wreck," *USA Today*, October 17, 2011.

3. "Gordon Smiley, a Driver, Killed at Indy," *New York Times*, May 16, 1982.

4. Loren Mooney, "This Kid Can Drive: Greg Moore IS CART's Youngest Three-Time Winner and Its Points Leader," *Sports Illustrated*, May 25, 1998; "CART Hit Hard by Fatal Crash of Popular and Talented Moore," *Sports Illustrated*, November 1, 1999.

63. BILL CHEESBOURG, ONE OF A KIND

1. Corky Simpson, "Racer Bill Cheesbourg Lived His Whole Life as a Winner," *Tucson Citizen*, November 7, 1995.

64. SUTTON RETIRED AFTER SEEING KENYON WRECK

1. Bill Poehler, "Legendary Racer Len Sutton, 81, Dies from Cancer Complications," *Statesman Journal* (Salem, OR), December 5, 2006.

2. Robin Miller, "Robin Miller on Mel Kenyon," video, *Racer.com*, March 2, 2015, http://www.racer.com/indycar/item/113967-racer-robin-miller-on-mel-kenyon.

3. Ibid.

65. BOYD SAW A LOT OF ACTION

1. Dorie Sweikert, *Along for the Ride: A Love Story* (Speedway, IN: C. Hungness, 1998).

2. "Johnny Boyd," National Midget Auto Racing Hall of Fame.

66. SPEED AND SAFETY MAY NOT MIX

1. Marshall Pruett, "The Next Safer IndyCar—Which Dan Wheldon Helped to Test," *PopularMechanics.com*, October 20, 2011, http://www.popularmechanics.com/cars/a7260/the-next-safer-indycar-which-dan-wheldon-helped-to-test/.

2. Bob Pockrass. "How Can Indy Car Be Safer?" *ABCNews.go.com*, August 24, 2015, http://abcnews.go.com/Sports/indycar-safer/story?id=33275496.

3. Joseph Siano, "Indy Cars Safest Ever, in Theory That Is," *New York Times,* May 22, 1991.

4. "Muncey, Hydro Racer, Killed in Acapulco Race," *New York Times,* October 20, 1981.

5. Comment to author.

STAN SUTTON is a member of the Indiana Sportswriters and Sportscasters Hall of Fame. During his career, Sutton worked for six newspapers in the Midwest, including twenty-five years with the *Louisville Courier-Journal*. He is the co-author of *Tales from the Indiana Hoosiers Locker Room* and *Tales from the 1980–81 Indiana Hoosiers*.

Printed and bound by CPI Group (UK) Ltd, Croydon, CR0 4YY

09/06/2025

14685937-0001